"The empowering message of *Rekindled Flame* will stir your heart, mind, and soul at every dimension. Your heart will burn with the revival fire of God's power; your mind will be transformed with the renewal of God's peace; and your soul will yearn for God's fullness to be realized in your life.

In other words, Steve Fry has written the 'psalm of revival,' calling us as believers to be awakened and ignited in our passion for righteousness."

JACK W. HAYFORD, LITT.D.
PASTOR/CHANCELLOR, THE CHURCH ON THE WAY,
THE KING'S SEMINARY, VAN NUYS, CALIFORNIA

"Steven has written a very honest book about life's most important quest. An important contribution to the field of pastoral spirituality that should be read by many."

DOUG BANISTER, SENIOR PASTOR,
FELLOWSHIP CHURCH, AUTHOR OF *SACRED QUEST*

"Steve Fry is a gifted communicator who knows how to bring people into God's presence through worship. *Rekindled Flame* is a timely word to the body of Christ, calling us back to bridal devotion to Jesus. For those praying for national spiritual awakening, this book is a must-read."

DR. BRUCE WILKINSON
AUTHOR OF THE BESTSELLING *THE PRAYER OF JABEZ*

"Amidst the hype, hoopla, and heartfelt pleas for revival, God has anointed a few, it seems, to be voices crying in the wilderness, 'Prepare ye the way….' Steve Fry is one of these uniquely gifted servants, and *Rekindled Flame* is that message for the church today. This book will drive you to your knees and fill your heart with an ache for the glories of Christ, who beckons you to walk with Him upon the highway of holiness that Steve so wonderfully lays before us."

TRICIA MCCARY RHODES
AUTHOR OF *CONTEMPLATING THE CROSS*

rekindled flame

THE PASSIONATE PURSUIT OF GOD

steve fry

Multnomah®Publishers *Sisters, Oregon*

REKINDLED FLAME
published by Multnomah Publishers, Inc.

© 2002 by Steven Fry
International Standard Book Number: 1-57673-791-8

Cover design by Chris Gilbert / UDG DesignWorks
Cover image by Photodisc

Scripture quotations are from:
The Holy Bible, New International Version © 1973, 1984 by International Bible
Society, used by permission of Zondervan Publishing House
New American Standard Bible (NASB) © 1960, 1977 by the Lockman Foundation
The Holy Bible, New King James Version (NKJV) © 1984 by Thomas Nelson, Inc.
The Holy Bible, King James Version (KJV)

Multnomah is a trademark of Multnomah Publishers, Inc.,
and is registered in the U.S. Patent and Trademark Office.
The colophon is a trademark of Multnomah Publishers, Inc.

Printed in the United States of America

For information:
MULTNOMAH PUBLISHERS, INC. • P.O. BOX 1720 • SISTERS, OR 97759

Library of Congress Cataloging-in-Publication Data

Fry, Steve, 1954–
    Rekindled flame / by Steven Fry.
    p. cm.
    ISBN 1-57673-791-8 (pbk.)
    1. God—Worship and love. I. Title.
    BV4817 .F79 2002
    248.3—dc21

                                        2001007867

02 03 04 05 06 07 08—10 9 8 7 6 5 4 3 2 1

To my wife, Nancy,
who has walked with me now
for over twenty-five years
in this journey of discovering
the wonder of God.

Most books are a team effort, and there have been many cooks in the kitchen stirring this pot. First I'd like to thank Tyler Freeny and Dru Heffington, who have served my wife, Nancy, and me in preparing this manuscript. I'd also like to thank Lela Gilbert and Tracy Sumner for their helpful editorial work, Bill Jensen for providing visionary oversight, and David Webb and Jennifer Gott, who nursed this book through its final stages.

I owe a large debt to the many hundreds in our old youth group who learned these principles together with us. I learned these truths not in isolation, but in community—in community with young people who felt they could honestly change their world for Christ.

I am greatly indebted to my sister Candace Strubhar, who has worked tirelessly as my publicist for the past year. I would also like to thank my mom and dad—who pray for us daily— and to the many leaders at Calvary Community Church, who in a season not long ago provided an environment in which worship could be expressed long before worship was as popular as it is today. That little congregation of 150 swelled to several thousand simply because men and women had an insatiable desire to worship God. I am the product of an environment in which worshiping God was supremely prized.

We have many prayer partners, and there are three in particular to whom I want to express singular gratitude for their intercession on our behalf: Tammy Alsup, Lynn Taff, and Libby Whittaker.

I also need to thank my children Cameron, Kelsey, and Caleigh. For many reasons, this book has been one of the hardest projects I have undertaken in quite a while. Trying to write and give leadership to a network of pastors while maintaining a "pedal to the metal" traveling schedule is no easy business. And this project took me from my children more than I would have thought possible when I started. They have been very patient with their father, and for their love and respect I am deeply grateful.

Lastly, the debt I owe to my wife, Nancy, is something only God can fully repay in His grace. I wrote this book during a year in which we had little administrative help. Nancy single-handedly managed the office, booked my schedule, shuttled the kids, and kept me sane—which was probably the hardest job of all. She is indeed my wonder woman!

preface

I once sat in the presence of a great man of godly character. As a successful pastor, he possessed a national reputation, with few peers his equal.

But as I looked into his soul that day, I saw a man whose heart had been hollowed out by his success. His face was drawn; his shoulders seemed to sag with the weight of countless expectations placed on him by others—and by himself. He had once known the simple joy of intimacy with the Lord, he told me. But now? The very ministry to which he had been called now drove him mercilessly to maintain his appearance as a man of purpose and vision.

Inside he was dying.

"I'm a victim of my own success," he muttered quietly. And he looked into my eyes searching for solace. Perhaps looking for his lost fire.

I sat there, still, hoping that I'd never slide to such a state.

But I did. As I put pen to paper here—and combed through many of the encounters I first had with God that etched these principles so indelibly into my heart—I realized that my flame of passion for God had flickered low.

In many ways, writing this book has been a journey back in time for me. Many of the principles I outline in these chapters were tooled out in the factory of my early years as a Christian leader. My keen appetite to know God was first whetted in high school. As a young pastor, I became even more ravenous for God, and the spiritual disciplines of worship, prayer, meditation in the Word, and cultivating sensitivity to His voice became the bedrock upon which I built my life and ministry. (Before we can truly understand how to worship God, we must know who He is. Read my book *I Am: The Unveiling of God* to learn more about God's character.)

But as is often the case, the "basics" get buried over time. God grants us success, prospers us, "enlarges our borders"— and soon our desire for a God-shaped heart slowly and imperceptibly wanes. We become sophisticated. Strong. Successful. All at once our power of perception replaces sensitivity to His Spirit. Our strength of ability replaces strength of character. And one day we turn around and realize that we've become victims of our success. Busy with the stuff of life. Comfortable in the place we've settled. No longer hungry for God, no longer desperate for His glory.

All too frequently I have bypassed the lovely wonders of God because I had so many promises to keep—so many people to please, so many programs to run, so many mountains to scale, so many battles to win. It seemed that I always had miles to go before I could rest in the sweet arms of Jesus and, like the disciple John, lay my head upon His chest.

Writing these pages has revealed to me my own stodgy heart, dulled by the incessant drives and demands generated by my own—often admirable—agendas. But at the end of the day, all we really have to give back to God is the heart for Him that He gave us in the first place. He, by His grace, ignites the flame of love for Him. Let us never undervalue the miracle that happens when God takes a person completely bent toward selfishness and kindles within him a flame of love for the God who made him. But how we tend that flame—that is the real issue of life.

He sets our hearts afire for Him, and at the end of our days, He sets our works afire to see if He can find Himself. That which looks like Him, smells like Him, sounds like Him—that is the gold that will remain on the day we stand before Him. And all the great movements and monuments of men so lauded now will be just so much dust in the wind.

May the fire of passion for God be rekindled in your heart, as it has in mine, as you read these pages. And may *He* once again become your unquenchable flame.

CHAPTER 1

Rekindling the Flame
to Know Him

Our restless spirits yearn for thee, wherever changeful lot is cast.
Glad when thy gracious smile we see, blest when our faith can hold thee fast.
BERNARD OF CLAIRVAUX

I sat staring at the piano, feeling as if I had lost my way—as if I'd lost my world. I was stunned by the shocking unraveling of what, up to that moment, had been a successful career.

Just a few months before, I had been relishing my role as one of the leading youth pastors on the West Coast. I had been blessed to steer the course of a youth group that had grown from a relative handful to more than seven hundred young people who honestly felt that they could change their world.

We had done it all. We had produced full-scale rock operas and Broadway-type musicals, had designed high-octane ministry training programs that mobilized mission teams to all parts of the globe, had launched discipleship groups across the Silicon Valley. We had seen God do miracles on the streets of San Francisco, had pioneered new models of youth programming, and had trained some of the finest youth leaders in the Bay Area. For nine years I had worked to come to this point: I was in demand as a youth specialist, and we were poised to take our youth ministry to a national level.

Then it all just blew up. Vanished.

Serious failures had surfaced in my leadership team, which took me completely by surprise. The complexity of the situation required wisdom that seemed to be beyond my grasp. Matters quickly worsened when I was blamed for others' mistakes that I had nothing to do with. I became the scapegoat. I felt betrayed. The youth leaders had distanced themselves from me, leaving me no choice but to resign my position. In a few short weeks, I was stripped to a Bible and one lone friend—my wife, Nancy. And there seemed to be nowhere to go.

I tried to make sense of it all. All kinds of emotions collided within me: bitterness toward the ones I felt had betrayed me, guilt over the way I had driven the youth group to accomplish *my* visions, fear of what all this might mean to my reputation, an aching emptiness at the thought of having worked so hard— only to apparently accomplish so little.

"It's just so futile!" I screamed to myself.

So I sat there in my living room, staring at the piano keys. Music had always been a comfort to me, but not now. The worship choruses and songs I had penned were like echoes in an empty hall.

I closed my eyes. Grief seemed to course through my fingers as I began to play. And somewhere from the deepest recesses of my soul, words began to flood my mind.

Just the time I feel that I've been caught
    in the mire of self
Just the time I feel my mind's been
    bought by worldly wealth.

That's how I felt—caught. Bought out. My world had collapsed, and as the moments passed, I gradually began to realize that it was no one's fault but mine. Once again, I had been seduced by the fast track, the lure of success, and the need to make my mark.

> I've run the race—yet set my pace and face a shattered
> soul....

I was the author of my misery, and I knew it. Worship had been an afterthought for a long time. Communion with God was running a distant second to climbing ladders. The feverish pace I had set had hooked me. Once again, I had become a driven man.

But all at once I felt a small drop of hope penetrate the thick despair that was suffocating my heart.

> That's when the breeze begins to blow—
>   I know the Spirit's call
> And all my worldly wandering just
>   melts into His love.

Jesus still loved me. Opportunistic, manipulative me. Self-centered, resentful me.

As overwhelmed as I was by what I had done—by the seeds of destruction I had sown because I cared more for my vision than for the sheep entrusted to me—I found myself suddenly buoyed by the simple truth that *Jesus still loved me.*

All at once it was as if I felt the Father's arms envelop me, and I began to cry out:

Oh, I want to know You more! Deep within my soul
    I want to know You, Oh, I want to know You
To feel Your heart and know Your mind
    Looking in Your eyes stirs up within me
Cries that say, "I want to know You!
    Oh, I want to know You more!"[1]

That was almost twenty years ago. In that span of time this song has perhaps been the most beloved song God has given me. Everywhere I go, people ask me to sing it. It seems to resonate within them, capturing their deepest passions for the Lord. This song has touched millions. It was forged in the crucible of rejection, in the wallows of loneliness. And it was written by a man who had lost everything he had worked for, only to discover that the greatest joy—the joy of knowing Him—can never be taken away.

Though we often find ourselves caught in the tug-of-war between our agendas and His desires, Jesus ever woos and pursues us, and the pull of His love is so much stronger than our intransigence. He is the Husband of our souls who, like the lover in Song of Solomon, strains to peer through the latticework just to get a glimpse of his estranged beloved, strives to catch our eye in a moment of mercy and remind us of the satisfaction we once knew (see Song of Songs 2:9).

Still, the pain of the heart that is no longer moored to His touch is agonizing.

GOD'S FINDING TIME

I realize now that those months of misery were what one of my mentors calls a "finding time," a season in which God graciously crowds us into a corner where we have to face ourselves and the utter emptiness that haunts our hearts.

I had lost my passion for Christ. I had forgotten that I once had the heart of a bride who loved Him with passion and followed Him with abandon. How had my heart become so cold? I couldn't recall a specific moment when I had turned my back on Him, but my passion for Him had dwindled to a faint flicker of what it once was.

The joy of His presence, the sweetness of His voice, had always genuinely satisfied me. And I knew that success was fleeting—the pursuit of a sense of personal significance nothing but a hollow odyssey. But knowing Him—desiring as David did just to behold the beauty of the Lord—was the one joy that never waned within me.

How can I now rekindle the flame of bridal devotion for Jesus? I asked myself.

As I looked back on the years leading up to this turning point, I realized that I had been slowly separating myself from God. Without meaning to or wanting to, I had inexorably wound my way down a path of unfaithfulness. For me, the pathway back to God began with remembering that my ultimate priority was to cultivate intimacy with Him.

As the days and all their incessant demands press on us, we must be ever vigilant to rekindle the flame of bridal passion for the Lord. Today it seems that more exists to distract us from this holy pursuit than at any other time in recent memory. The church is being distracted to death; and the distractions hit us from all directions. We are overloaded with e-mails, cable channels, cell phones, and hours on the freeway. New technologies allow us to be in more relationships, but often we find ourselves spending inordinate amounts of time adjusting our relational world, trying to make room on an already full plate.

Because our society creates environments in which people feel disconnected and alienated, a number of people are on the hunt for meaning and personal significance—PWAs (People With Agendas), as one of my pastor friends calls them. PWAs often enter into relationships more as a means of determining their self-worth than of simply fostering friendships, and in so doing end up using people without even knowing it.

Then there are all those opportunities afforded our children: ballet classes for the five-year-old, drama for the ten-year-old, soccer matches, basketball games, violin lessons. Sometimes these things seem to reduce parents to nothing more than veritable taxi services. And when we finally get our kids home, we have to monitor their on-line chat rooms, scrutinize the content of their television programs, and watchdog their Web surfing.

Bosses to please, new gadgets to test, kids to shuttle…

All this can leave us feeling utterly spent, and that's when some of the subtlest distractions present themselves—those innocuous amusements we pursue in an effort to revitalize our numb souls. But golf courses, cineplexes, and shopping malls cannot replenish a depleted spirit.

The most insidious distractions of all are our own needs: the need to feel significant, the need to be successful, the need to be esteemed, the need to feel whole. These needs are subtle distractions precisely because they are so legitimate. And because we have these needs, we can find ourselves pursuing God more for our sake than for His.

When that happens, it's time to make some changes.

WANTING CHRIST FOR CHRIST'S SAKE

A few years ago, my family and I moved from San Jose, California, where we had lived for most of our lives, to Nashville, Tennessee. By that time, I had been involved in the Christian communications industry for a number of years. Many of the record companies were moving to Nashville in the early nineties, so we migrated there as well.

Once we settled, I had the opportunity to huddle with some executives from one of the more well-known Christian labels. They knew about my work and were interested in doing a recording with me. When they asked what kind of project I'd like to do, I told them that I wanted to write a worship musical that focused on the character of God—a collection of worship songs that would celebrate the many facets of His wonder.

The executives' response was surprisingly cool. They told me that they would like to help but that, frankly, most believers would not buy an album about God. According to their demographic studies, such a project would not appeal to most Christians. I thought it strange that a recording that celebrated the very One who is our author of life would hold so little appeal to the average believer. But, of course, what did I know? They were the executives, and I was simply a songwriter.

A few months later, I had another encounter that mirrored

the one with the record company. I was in the process of writing my first book and met with the editor who had been assigned to finesse my manuscript. I knew that he was one of the best editors in the business. Having worked in the past for some of the largest publishing houses, he had his finger on the pulse of the Christian marketplace. He asked me what I wanted to write about, and I told him the same thing I'd told the record company brass.

"I want to write about God!" I said. "I want to take snapshots of the many wonders of His character and just focus on Him."

"I'd like to help you write that kind of a book," he replied. "In fact, the Christian market desperately needs that kind of book. But honestly, the average Christian is not going to buy a book about God."

It sounded like the same song and dance to me, but then he explained himself. "The only way you can get the average believer to read a book about God is to somehow show them how God benefits *them*," he said.

I sat there stunned. It wasn't that I fully disagreed, for I knew that most people pursue God because they see Him as the One who satisfies their desires. But my editor's words rattled me. Something didn't sit well.

As I reflected on those two encounters, I realized that if these media mavens were giving me accurate information, then there was something gravely wrong in the church. *Have we become so obsessed with ourselves,* I asked myself, *that we subconsciously perceive God as existing for us—and not us for Him?*

In truth, many of us want to get to know God so we can be

better parents, so we can be more successful businesspeople, so we can feel whole. Even spiritual leaders sometimes pursue God more from the desire for ministry success than simply the desire for God Himself.

The Word of God, as always, provides the necessary connective. In the book of Philippians, we catch a glimpse into Paul's hunger for the Lord when he exclaims, "I want to know Christ and the power of his resurrection and the fellowship of sharing in his sufferings" (3:10). When we read this verse, we don't get the sense that Paul wanted to know God in order to be a better leader, a more effective church planter, or more highly esteemed by his colleagues. He wanted Christ for Christ's sake, period!

This sentiment captures the essence of true bridal affection that we as a church should have for Christ. It is a craving for Jesus, a hunger centered on Him, not on our needs. That many of us have been shanghaied by what Christopher Lasch described as a "culture of narcissism"[2]—and have unsuspectingly adopted a self-serving form of Christianity—can be seen in the weariness many believers feel and the degree to which we are so easily distracted from our passionate pursuit of God.

THE QUIET PLACE OF THE HEART

In his book *The Way of the Heart,* Henri Nouwen addresses proper focus on Jesus Christ:

> What needs to be guarded is the life of the Spirit
> within us.... It is not so strange that many ministers

have become burnt out cases, people who say many
words and share many experiences, but in whom the
fire of God's Spirit has died and from whom not much
more comes forth than their own blind, petty ideas
and feelings…. Our first and foremost task is faithfully
to care for the inward fire so that when it is really
needed it can offer warmth and light to lost travelers.[3]

Guarding that inner fire is the challenge of twenty-first-
century life. The drivenness that can so quickly quench the
flame of intimacy with God can only be expunged by discovering what Catherine of Siena called the "cell of the heart."

Catherine was alluding to the monasteries of her day. They
were places where men and women could shut out the distractions of their world and focus solely on cultivating intimacy
with God. But she saw that a person needn't cloister himself
away to center himself on communion with Christ, for that
place of communion need not be farther away than one's own
heart, that inner sanctum that belongs only to the Bridegroom
of our souls. An inner habitation where deep calls unto deep,
where in the silence and the solitude of communion with our
Beloved we touch the eternal and walk in the rest and peace that
is to mark our lives in this Roller Derby world.

To tend this "inner monastery," we must learn the supreme
value of unplugging from the cacophonous buzz of life's many
distractions.

S. D. Gordon, one of D. L. Moody's contemporaries, tells
this story:

A gentleman was asked by an artist friend of some note to come to his home, and see a painting just finished. He went at the time appointed, was shown by the attendant into a room which was quite dark and left there. He was much surprised, but quietly awaited developments. After perhaps 15 minutes his friend came into the room with a cordial greeting, and took him up to the studio to see the painting, which was greatly admired. Before he left, the artist said laughingly, "I suppose you thought it queer to be left in that dark room so long." "Yes," the visitor said. "I did." "Well," his friend replied, "I knew that if you came into my studio with the glare of the street in your eyes you could not appreciate the fine coloring of the picture. So I left you in the dark room till the glare had worn out of your eyes."[4]

In the dark and alone: the only way the visitor could appreciate such exquisite art.

In the same way, God desires to get us alone with Him. Not just the aloneness of a brief quiet time, but an inner solitude that can be known even in our busiest moments. This is a solitude born in a heart that focuses solely on Jesus. It's a rest found when we see how passionately God wants us.

WANTED ... BY GOD!

Scripture is the record of God's passion for us. It is the record of a God who wanted to walk with Adam in the cool of the day, a

God whose passion for Enoch—who delighted in God's every step—was so great that in a moment of divine delight He raptured Enoch away.

He is a God who allowed Abraham to wait and wait for his promised son Isaac—perhaps simply for the joy of repeated encounters with His servant, or perhaps for the joy of unwrapping His promise over twenty-five years, to reveal layer after precious layer to a man who pursued intimacy with his God.

He is a God who dares to place Himself against every conceivable pleasure—wealth, fame, sexual desire—and says that He is the greatest reward of all (Genesis 15:1).

He is a God who pursues a swindler like Jacob, a God who wrestles the man until dawn even though He could have crippled him in an instant. And why? So He could bring Jacob to a place of such absolute dependence that his heart would be forever linked with His own.

He's a God who called Moses from the fire and whose word became such a fire within him that Moses' own soul thereafter could burn for nothing less than face-to-face intimacy with Him.

He's a God who met with a young shepherd in the dark recesses of the night, inspiring in him song after delightful song, forever ruining him for the mere achievements of earthly giants.

And He's a God who wanted us with such unquenchable desire that He became a seed in a woman's womb, the smallest entity of life, in order to rescue us from our sin.

To be *needed* is a tonic for the soul that feels neglected, cast off, discarded. But to be *wanted?* Now there's a tantalizing elixir that can satiate the deepest yearnings of the heart. To be the object of another's desire, the sole focus of a lover's affection. To be wanted for no other reason save the adorer's passion to know us and be known by us.

To be desired not for what we have done, nor for what we have earned. To be wanted not for what we may have to offer another, nor for the services we might be able to render.

To be wanted for no other reason than the pleasure of another to simply lavish affection upon us. To be afforded the exquisite delight of revealing yourself in the embrace of unconditional love.

To be desired for no other reason but that you *as you* are immeasurably valuable.

To be wanted simply because you are of inestimable worth—that is heaven!

That taste of heaven is known only in the arms of Jesus, only in our times alone with Him where face-to-face intimacy is cultivated in worship.

Chapter 2

The Danger of staying in the outer court

Shut your door upon you and call unto Jesus your love.
When Jesus is nigh all goodness is nigh and nothing seems hard;
but when he is not nigh all things are hard.

Thomas à Kempis

So often, the things that tug at our hearts and distract us from the pursuit of intimacy with God are good things—important responsibilities, significant commitments, even God-given visions. But these *good* things can so easily crowd out the *best* thing—communion with Jesus. Over time we can find ourselves not quite as sensitive to His voice, not quite as quick to obey, not quite as hungry for His Word.

In my life it has often been the well-intentioned plans and noble aspirations that have siphoned away my passion for God. Early on in my ministry, I discovered just how easily my communion with the Lord could be compromised.

I had finished preaching one evening. I supposed that the meeting had gone well, but I really couldn't tell. My emotions felt dull. A creeping numbness seemed to choke any satisfaction I might have otherwise enjoyed from what had been a string of successes. Envisioning great undertakings came easily for me, and passion for ministry seemed to course through my veins.

With the zeal that comes with youth I had filled my calendar with all kinds of projects: outreaches, upreaches, inreaches. The fast track toward becoming one of the largest youth groups on the West Coast was exhilarating. And though it felt at times like we were spinning twenty-five hours a day, I was having a great time. The frenetic pace was addicting, and life for my wife and me seemed like a straight shot to the moon.

It didn't take long, though, for the pace to catch up with me. The helter-skelter schedule we were keeping slowly drained my enthusiasm. At the ripe old age of twenty-two—and as a "veteran" of four years in youth ministry—I was exhausted. Anyone looking at our program would have thought we were surfing a wave of success, but I was dying inside. I was so driven in ministry, yet so driven from God.

I was beyond fatigue; I was frustrated and burned out. Finally, at a point of sheer desperation, I got on my face in the small study of our condominium and cried out to God. He nudged me to read Ezekiel 44. As I read, I quickly realized that a message in this passage was about to change my life:

> "They may serve in my sanctuary, having charge of the gates of the temple…and stand before the people and serve them. But because they served them in the presence of their idols…therefore I have sworn with uplifted hand that they must bear the consequences of their sin…. *They are not to come near to serve me as priests.*" (vv. 11–13, emphasis added)

Serve the people but not come near Him? As I read those words, I shuddered. I knew enough about the temple and its rituals to understand the difference between the outer court, where the priests served the people, and the inner court, where the priests ministered to God.

The outer court was the area where the priests assisted the people as they offered their sacrifices. It was necessary ministry, but often exhausting. The inner court was the place where a priest, when it was his turn in the rotation, would come and offer incense on the altar before the Lord. To settle one's heart before the presence of the Lord, to "minister to Him," was sweet joy to the priests.[1] But these priests in Ezekiel 44 were forbidden to enter the inner court, the place where they could enjoy the presence of the Lord.

As I meditated on this chapter, it was as if the Lord spoke to the deepest part of my heart and said, "You know that I love you and that I have called you and given you gifts and abilities. But like these priests, you have been serving Me in the presence of an idol. That idol is the god of vision and ministry. You have become so enamored with your ministry, and all that you are doing, that you have neglected intimacy with Me. Because I love you, I will not take your ministry from you. But if you continue on the path you are on, I will give you over to your ministry, and you will no longer have the joy of My presence."

A shock pulsed through my soul. The words *I will give you over to your ministry* had a ring of danger about them. It was as if I was about to be given over to the control of an alien force. I realized that I was flirting with disaster. But I also knew that ministry to people in the "outer court" was so satisfying in the short run that I might not know when I had crossed the line where I would find myself consumed with people and not with God. I did not want to risk banishment to a place where I could minister to people but could no longer taste intimacy with Him.

I realized then and there that the most important ministry any of us has is our ministry to God. The idea of ministering to God can at first seem to infringe on His self-sufficiency. To suggest that God somehow needs our ministry portrays Him as lacking something, which, of course, He does not. Only a God who is fully sufficient within Himself can be trusted to meet *all* our needs.

Yet God desires ministry from us. What does it mean to minister to God? Simply put, it means to cultivate intimacy with Him, to set aside devoted time for Him, to focus on Him and reflect on His beauty. To minister to the Lord is to *worship* Him.

God's desire for our worship is not the craving of an egotistical king, nor the demand of a celestial power broker. Rather, it is the yearning of a Bridegroom who wants us more than our deepest need to be wanted. A Lover whose pleasure is to give Himself away, and who has designed us to be like Himself—finding pleasure in giving *ourselves* away. But before we can give ourselves to others, we need to give ourselves to God by worshiping Him. And it is only as we give ourselves away in abandoned worship that we can ever know this God who gives Himself away.

WHAT IS WORSHIP?

Worship is the doorway to all other holy passions. It is the fountainhead of all ministry. But what exactly is worship? Perhaps describing it will help us better define it.

Worship means having a heart that delights in obeying God, even when obedience calls for sacrifice.

One of the first times we find the word *worship* in Scripture, it is not used against the backdrop of some joyous Davidic celebration or a rousing dance celebrating the defeat of an enemy. It is used when the Lord tells Abraham to sacrifice his beloved Isaac. Isaac was the son of promise, the fulfillment of a twenty-five-year wait. But in Genesis 22, God tells Abraham to slay the very expression of His own affection toward him.[2]

This was a crisis. Not only was Abraham called to kill the apple of his eye, but his confidence in God's word and character itself was being tested. God's love had fulfilled the promise of a son; was it now hatred that demanded his son's death? Abraham must have questioned what kind of God he worshiped.

Yet Abraham saddled his donkey and took Isaac, and together they began their journey to Mount Moriah. When his servants asked him where he was going, Abraham replied, "The lad and I are going up that mountain to *worship*" (see v. 5).

To sing? No.

To dance? No.

To celebrate? No.

They were going to worship.

In the face of sheer agony, Abraham obeyed God. Somewhere deep in the hidden nooks of his heart, Abraham maintained his trust in God, and herein we find perhaps one of the greatest definitions of worship in Scripture: Worship is a heart of sacrificial devotion, a heart that steadfastly obeys, even in the face of the deepest sorrow.

Worship is shaped by two attitudes: reverence and intimacy.

In the Hebrew lexicon, one of the primary words for worship is *shachah,* which is used 170 times in the Hebrew Bible. In her book *Prophetic Worship,* Vivian Hibbert describes the literal meaning of the verbal root of this word as "the act of falling down and groveling, even wallowing on the ground before royalty (2 Samuel 14:22; 1 Kings 1:16) or deity (Exodus 34:8; 2 Samuel 12:20)."[3]

Another Hebrew word, although not used as often in Scripture, adds the sheen of intimacy to our picture of worship. It is the word *sharath,* and it is used in Ezekiel 44:15–16 to convey our ministry to the Lord. Ministering to the Lord in this passage does not mean the simple fulfillment of liturgical duties.[4] It means focusing on Him.

Let me use my marriage to illustrate this idea of *focus.* Sometimes when my wife needs my attention and I find myself distracted, I can easily give her one ear instead of both. When she recognizes that I am doing that, she chides me and says, "Now, focus on me for a minute." The call to minister to the Lord is the call of a spouse who desires her mate's focus, not a boss who simply wants compliance.

One of the primary Greek words for worship is *proskuneo,* used over fifty times in the New Testament. It connotes both a deep reverence—like a dog licking his master's hand—as well as intimacy, because it literally means "to kiss the hand toward." In our day, a good parallel would be the act of blowing a kiss.[5]

Whether the word *worship* causes us to imagine Abraham resolving to sacrifice the object of his affection to God or think of David dancing wildly before the Lord, one inescapable truth emerges: Worship fuels our passion for God.

THE PERIL OF NEGLECTING OUR MINISTRY TO GOD

The Lord is actually addressing two groups of priests in Ezekiel 44, and it is to the first group that He essentially says, "You may serve in my sanctuary, but you *are not to come near to serve Me as priests*" (vv. 11–13, emphasis added).

Some background may be helpful at this point. In Moses' time the tabernacle was composed of two areas: the outer and the inner courts. In the outer court stood two furnishings: the bronze altar and the bronze laver (actually made from the copper mirrors of the Israelite women and used by the priests for ceremonial washing). The inner court was made up of two chambers: the Holy Place and the Most Holy Place.

When the worshiper entered the tabernacle area, he would approach the altar. It was upon this altar that he offered sacrifices. The outer court, then, was where the priests served the people by assisting them in their sacrificial offerings.

The inner court was where a priest, when it was his turn, came to offer incense on the altar of incense. The incense is analogous not only to our prayer but also to our worship. The altar was situated in front of the veil that separated the Holy Place from the Most Holy Place. Behind the veil was the ark of the covenant, which represented the throne and presence of God. The great joy of the priests, of course, was to be able to come into that inner court and "minister to the Lord."[6]

What God was essentially telling these priests was that they could no longer come into the inner court to enjoy His presence. But why?

First, they served God in the presence of their idols.

An idol is anything that consistently distracts us from God, any-thing that motivates us outside of simply glorifying God. Of course, our idols today are much more sophisticated. We would not be caught bowing to gods of metal and stone. Mine was the idol of vision. For others, their idol is their children. Still others idolize career. Some worship their talents; some worship their pasts.

Many dynamics shape our decisions—for example, concern over what people think of us, anxiety about our future, frustra-tion over lost time and squandered opportunities. When these kinds of attitudes and fears consistently shape our motives, it can indicate idolatry lurking within. These are self-serving forces and are often hard to detect.

For example, if I am motivated to place a friendly call to someone simply to make sure that I remain on his or her good side, my reputation has become idolatrous to me. I am more concerned with preserving my standing in that person's eyes than I am with his or her welfare. Thus, I am making a decision based not on what glorifies God, but on what will protect my backside.

Second, there is a sense in which these priests began to view the temple as existing for the people's sake and not God's.

This is a deceptive temptation because on the face of it, it is a noble thing to strive to meet people's needs. After all, God Himself delights in meeting our needs. But we cross a danger-ous line when meeting the needs of others supersedes hearing the word of the Lord.

We need to remember that God knows what people need far better than we do. He even knows how and when to instigate programs to meet those needs. The issue is this: *Who or what motivates us?* Does that local congregation exist to meet people's needs, or does it exist for the glory of God? Of course, these two drives needn't be set against each other, for God is our Father and He wants to meet our needs far more than we want them met. But we need to make sure that our ministries are driven not by the needs of others, but rather by the Word of the Lord.

We can apply the same principle to our families. We should ask ourselves if our families exist for the individual needs of the family members or for the glory of God. If we truly want to glorify God, then we will strive to respond to His direction regarding our families.

Third, the root sin of these priests was pride.
We too must deal with the root sin of pride. Pride does not have to manifest itself in arrogance or self-centeredness to be destructive. In fact, perhaps the most destructive workings of pride are the less apparent ones. For example, neglecting our inner-court ministry to God can be the result of sincere but misguided pursuits of ministry. We become so involved with outer-court ministry that we find ourselves exhausted, the inner fire of holy joy snuffed out by our own visions.

At the end of the day, pouring oneself out for the needs of others without spending commensurate time with God is an expression of pride. Such an omission is saying, in effect, that though we have not spent time in the presence of the Lord, we still believe we have something meaningful to offer others. Pride provokes us to believe that we actually have something to give apart from what the Lord breathes into us as we wait upon Him.

The great turn-of-the-century expositor F. B. Meyer reproves us this way: "Try breathing out three times without breathing in."[7] What he meant was that the exhale of ministry is only as life giving as our inhale of worship.

Fourth, they allowed the uncircumcised and foreigners into the temple.

At first this problem doesn't seem as obvious as the others, but the Lord rebuked them for this nonetheless. So what application does this have for us? Certainly this doesn't mean that we should distance ourselves from unbelievers or bar them from encountering Christ's loving presence in our gatherings. Remember, the apostle Paul clearly expected unbelievers to be present in believers' gatherings (see 1 Corinthians 14:24–25).

But we can draw an interesting application from this reference. These priests had become so used to allowing the uncircumcised to have expression within the temple that it had become quite commonplace. Those of us who are in roles of spiritual leadership can cross a line here without knowing it. It is so easy for us to allow those who are "uncircumcised in heart"—untested in their character, unbroken in their attitudes—to function in roles of spiritual responsibility and authority.

One of the great snares to which spiritual leaders fall prey is that of delegating based on talent and ability instead of character. When we are faced with the pressure to keep the church moving forward, we can find ourselves delegating responsibility in order to fill glaring needs.

Take the worship leader who has just lost his best bass player. Having grown accustomed to having a hot band, this worship leader now finds himself dreading Sunday worship services because he has lost one of his best players and thus a great deal of musical quality. He fears that this will leave the congregation dissatisfied, which can indirectly reflect negatively on his leadership.

So when he discovers that a newcomer to the church is an accomplished bass player, he moves quickly to secure his services often in the name of "providing an outlet for that person's ministry" without assessing heart attitudes such as humility. Adding the player to the band may work out well, or it may backfire. Either way, though, it exposes a motivation of pride in the worship leader, which inhibits the blessing of God.

Improper delegation can, over time, cause leaders to lose their passion for God and their fire for ministry, leaving them feeling banished to the outer court.

Fifth, the priests simply neglected their ministry to God.
No doubt they must have carried on some formal execution of their priestly duties within the inner court, but they no longer encountered the Lord of glory there. We come back to a snare we discussed earlier: distraction. We can become so caught up with the everyday worries of life—desperately trying to find little pleasures here and there that can take our minds off our

ever-increasing anxieties—that we neglect our relationship with the Lord. Simple neglect is one of the most formidable challenges, because the reasons for the neglect are usually so sane and understandable.

Of course, the Lord is gracious, patient, and very slow to anger. As the psalmist said, He understands that our frame is as dust (Psalm 103:14). He knows the demands that tend to deplete us, and He will work with us over and over again to wean us from our dependence on outer-court activity.

But if we stubbornly refuse to tend to our first priority—our ministry to God—then He will let us taste ministry without joy, service without satisfaction, and responsibility without rejoicing.

entering the inner court

God answers the diligent seeker, not the casual inquirer.

JOY DAWSON

The evening before Mother's Day, while the rest of the family was tucked away in bed, I prepared a special breakfast for my wife. For seven long years we had tried to have children, and then God blessed us with two back to back. With a couple of toddlers now to our credit, I wanted to honor Nancy with flowers, freshly squeezed California orange juice, and melt-in-your-mouth cinnamon rolls, all presented on our best china in the dining room.

Well, the best-laid plans…

During the night, both of the kids had us up every hour. You know the routine: bad dreams, drinks of water, earaches, endless pats on the back. By morning, Nancy and I were exhausted. Still, we dragged ourselves out of bed and gamely tried to enjoy the little feast I had prepared. As we sat at the dining room table, our kids, now both wide-awake (it's amazing how kids can tussle all night, then rise full of mischief by early morning), were screaming and fighting in the next room.

As I poured Nancy's orange juice, she looked with blood-shot eyes across the table and said, "I want to thank you for making me a mother!"

Our little moment of intimacy that morning was being chilled by the results of another little moment of intimacy. The irony of it! As my friend Pastor Don Finto says, "Intimacy produces babies, but babies can destroy intimacy." Parents know this only too well. The amorous memories of passionate evenings quickly fade with three o'clock feedings.

There is a similar kind of irony in our communion with the Lord. As we spend time adoring Him and listening to Him, He gives us ideas, summons us to partner with Him in ministry, and calls us to reach out to others. We enthusiastically tackle new projects and launch great programs, programs that are not *our* efforts but *His* initiatives. But it doesn't take long for those "babies" to impede our ongoing communion with Christ.

How can we maintain a life of intimacy with God? How can we find a rhythm between outer-court ministry to people and inner-court ministry to God?

THE JOY OF THE INNER COURT

In chapter 2, I talked about a group of priests to whom God said that they could serve in His sanctuary, but were not to come near to serve Him as priests (Ezekiel 44:10–14). To the second group, identified as the sons of Zadok, God says of these:

> "'[They] who faithfully carried out the duties of my sanctuary when the Israelites went astray from me, are to come near to minister before me; they are to stand before me to offer sacrifices of fat and blood, declares the Sovereign LORD. They alone are to enter my sanc-

tuary; they alone are to come near my table to minister before me....

"'When they enter the gates of the inner court,
they are to wear linen clothes; they must not wear any
woolen garment while ministering at the gates of the
inner court.... They are to wear linen turbans on their
heads and linen undergarments around their waists.
They must not wear anything that makes them per-
spire.'" (vv. 15–18)

Herein lies the great joy for us as believers. As Peter said, we
are all priests (1 Peter 2:9), and as such we all have the same call
and privilege to minister unto the Lord. Indeed, that is our most
important ministry, for we have nothing to give to others without first receiving from Him in the place of worship. Our ministry to one another in the body of Christ is essential, our
ministry to those enslaved by sin, critical. But our number one
ministry is to God Himself.

That is the joy God gave these sons of Zadok—and the joy
He wants us to know. It is the joy of coming into His presence
and ministering to Him.

But how do we prepare ourselves to minister to God in the
inner court? In much the same way the priests prepared themselves.

TAKING OFF THE WOOL, PUTTING ON THE LINEN

The first thing the priests were told to do to prepare for the inner
court was to take off the wool garments they were wearing,

which were standard for outer-court service. In Moses' day, the tabernacle was the central worship facility, and it served well over a million people. On any given day, someone entering it would be met with a cacophony of noise from hundreds of people and from scores of animals about to be sacrificed on the brazen altar. The priests wore wool garments while assisting the people with their sacrifices. After a day's work, their garments would have been pretty messy—spattered with mud, blood, and animal excrement.

Ministering to people in the outer court was necessary but messy business. And as we've seen, the joy came for the priests when it was their turn to burn incense on the altar in the inner court. But entering that place required certain preparations. A priest could not haphazardly enter God's presence.

The robes the priests wore would not only be soiled and sweaty, but also being made of wool wouldn't allow the priests' skin to breathe. For that reason, the priests were commanded to dress themselves in linen, a lightweight fabric that allows the body to cool. The Lord required linen garments because He did not want the priests to wear anything that would cause them to sweat (Ezekiel 44:17–18).

Neither does God want us to "sweat" in His presence. Removing the wool and putting on the linen speaks to how we prepare our hearts when coming before the Lord in the act of worship. "Putting on the linen" has two applications for us.

Celebrating God's grace

Linen signifies "the righteousness of the saints" (see Revelation 19:8). This is the righteousness that comes from Christ, the righteousness that is ours by faith in Him and bestowed on us by His grace. The linen, therefore, speaks of that place of security we have because of our standing of righteousness before the Lord: where we are no longer suffocating under the awful weight of guilt and condemnation, where we can spiritually breathe.

We need to constantly remind ourselves of our standing before the Father, which can be easy or hard to do depending on how we feel at a given time. But it doesn't matter whether or not we *feel* righteous. We need to state our standing in Christ by faith.

God has declared us righteous, which means we can confess sin in His presence, rather than confessing as a means to obtain His presence. We often labor under the erroneous view that we must stand apart from the Lord until we have gone through sufficient cleansing through the confession of sin. Such a view conditions us to value the quality of our performance and further etches the groove of insecurity into our minds. Understanding that God accepts us unconditionally frees us to view confession in a different way.

This is important to grasp, for unless we truly understand grace we will always be insecure in our worship. Apart from grace, our desire to worship will wane. There are two reasons for this: Either our acts of worship will deteriorate into works designed to earn God's favor, or our zest for worship will be blunted over time because we feel insecure before a holy God.

Grace makes lifetime worshipers.

Quieting our hearts

Putting on the linen also speaks to the process of quieting our hearts and minds and allowing them to "breathe." So many of us do not allow ourselves to settle into the rest that is ours in Christ.

The garden of rest is tended by quiet hearts. Indeed, the psalmist calls us to "Be still, and know that [He] is God" (Psalm 46:10). The word *know* in this context connotes experience. It is the same word often used in Scripture to convey marital intimacy. But we cannot know God this way until we have stilled our hearts before Him. Granted, the text speaks of a quiet heart that trusts God in the midst of chaos and conflict. But there is yet another application for us: a stilling of the heart that sensitizes our spirit to God.

How often we come to times of solitude with God only to find our minds crammed full of *stuff*—obligations, people's expectations, deadlines, e-mails to read and write, children to tend to. We have 101 agendas, from feeding the dog to pleasing the boss—*stuff* that clutters our minds and diverts our focus.

To "take off the wool" is to spend the initial moments of our quiet time with God slowly eliminating all these distractions.

When preparing ourselves for meaningful communion with the Lord, it is necessary to undergo a sort of detox of the heart and mind. It is helpful when "removing the wool" to follow these steps:

1. *Enter His gates with thanksgiving* (see Psalm 100:4). Express gratitude for what God provides.
2. *Enter His courts with praise.* Think of the various attributes of His character and speak them out in prayer.
3. *Write down the things you have to do and the commitments you've made.* Allow yourself a few minutes just to do a

"brain dump." As you write down each thing, imagine yourself putting them in God's "pending" tray, and relinquish them to Him. If any item seems pressing to you, ask the Lord to give you wisdom and grace to follow through at the appropriate time. But resolve not to "sweat" about anything in His presence.

4. *Simply say to your mind, "Quiet!"* There is no end to the whirling wheels of needs and "oughtas." Satan himself is just too willing to keep feeding our minds with clutter. A friend of mine calls it the "demon of ideas." At some point we have to be ruthless with our minds and "tighten the belt" of our imaginations (1 Peter 1:13). We need to ignore any mental interruptions and intentionally focus on Jesus.

Now we are ready to offer ourselves afresh to God by submitting ourselves to Him (James 4:7) and offering ourselves "to God...as instruments of righteousness" (Romans 6:13).

Yielding to the Spirit

In his letter to the Philippians, the apostle Paul says that we "worship *by* the Spirit of God" (3:3, emphasis added). For Paul, a relationship with the person of the Holy Spirit was not a static arrangement. In fact, he did not see it as mere empowerment, for to do so would be to relegate the Spirit to a force or an idea. No, Paul's language stresses the *indwelling* of the Spirit in the lives of believers—individually and corporately.[1]

To Paul, a relationship with the Holy Spirit was dynamic, implying a constant interaction with Him as counselor, comforter, and coach. Paul viewed yielding to Him as a moment-by-moment cultivation of sensitivity to His voice. When the apostle enjoins the Ephesians to "be filled with the Spirit" (Ephesians 5:18), he is actually saying be continually filled or under the control of the Spirit.

Like a virtuoso guitarist constantly tuning his instrument during a concert so as to elicit accurate pitch, so we are to constantly "tune ourselves" to the Spirit. Failing to understand our need to be ever yielding to the Spirit's control is to flirt with presumption, meaning that we think we are cruising in the Spirit when in fact we are functioning in the flesh. This is why David prayed, "Save me from the sin of presumption" (see Psalm 19:13, NKJV).

Presumption can seriously compromise our worship. Blaise Pascal writes as if God Himself were speaking to us on this issue: "I showed you My glory…but you could not bear such great glory without falling into the sin of presumption. You wanted to make yourself your own center and do without My help."[2]

For example, we may not think we need God's help in crafting appropriate worship styles, but we do. Without a sensitivity to the Spirit, we can reduce worship to an experience that fits comfortably within the parameters of our preferences. In other words, styles of worship that tend to nourish our own spirituality or that coincide with the ways we view God become our norm. This is understandable, but it sets the risky precedent of reducing worship—and our concept of God—to what makes us comfortable.

We prepare our hearts to worship by quieting our hearts and minds so that we can hear the Spirit. One of the desert fathers called the Old Peasant of Ars put it this way: "I don't say anything to God. I just sit and look at Him and let Him look at me."[3]

Once we have quieted our hearts, we can fulfill Paul's call to "offer [our] bodies as living sacrifices, holy and pleasing to God—this is [our] spiritual act of worship" (Romans 12:1). Once our minds have been cleansed, we can sense the tender nudgings of the Spirit and realize what according to the apostle Paul is present reality: "We have the mind of Christ" (1 Corinthians 2:16).

WORSHIPING IN THE SPIRIT

Christ's encounter with the woman at the well in John 4—a passage containing some of the most foundational insights on worship in the entire Word—underscores this dynamic of yielding to and worshiping in the Holy Spirit. In this familiar exchange, the subject of appropriate worship surfaces. Jesus makes two statements that, if we understand them, will revolutionize our approach to worship.

The first thing Jesus says is that the Father seeks worshipers (vv. 21–23). The Father, Scripture says, seeks two kinds of people: intercessors (Ezekiel 22:30) and worshipers. He doesn't seek evangelists, spiritual leaders, great strategists, or revivalists. He seeks those who give themselves to prayer and worship, because He knows that if He has pray-ers and praisers everything else necessary for His work will be released.

Christ also tells the Samaritan woman that those who would worship the Father must "worship [Him] in spirit and in truth" (v. 24). This phrase is richly layered theologically, and many astute definitions have been offered to explain it. Let me offer just a couple of practical angles from which to view this.

To worship in spirit can be understood in many different ways. It is to acknowledge, for example, that worship is a *spiritual* enterprise, suggesting the "otherness" of the One we worship. But one helpful way to apply this verse is to see it as a call to yield to the person of the Holy Spirit, thereby allowing Him to guide our worship experience before the Lord.

To worship in truth, I suggest, is to worship *with integrity.* That is, we should strive by His grace and in His spirit to emulate the object of our worship. For example, we cannot *truthfully* sing that great hymn "Great Is Thy Faithfulness" if we are being disloyal to a brother or sister in Christ. And we cannot praise Him for His power if we are not yielding our lives to Him or allowing Him to enable us to withstand temptation.

Paul tells us in 1 Corinthians 2:11 that the Spirit knows the mind of the Father. That being the case, the Holy Spirit knows which precise expressions of worship from my life bring Him the most pleasure. When we are yielded to Him, He can whisper to us those expressions of praise and worship the Father wants to receive at different times. For example, the Spirit may prompt us to prostrate ourselves before the Lord in awe of His holiness. At another time, He may provoke us to be silent. At still another time, He may lead us to stand up and shout in triumph.

To think of worship this way—that God desires to receive a variety of expressions of my devotion and affection—seems at first rather frivolous. It is almost like picturing God as a whimsical Sovereign that we need to size up at any given time in order to ascertain which postures of praise may tickle His fancy. But that substantially misses the point.

Yielding to the Spirit in the act of worship has nothing to do with any divine whimsy. Rather, it is the safeguard that keeps us from reducing worship to what we're used to or comfortable with and consequently expressing worship according to what pleases us more than what honors Him.

God is bigger than any of us, bigger than any one denomination, bigger than any one cultural expression. The Holy Spirit wants us to see God in His fullness and wants to open us to all manner of biblically based gestures of praise and worship.

Because God delights in a variety of worship expressions, He wants us to become sensitive to His voice so that we may know *how* He wants us to worship each time we come before Him. That He desires such sensitivity on our part has nothing whatever to do with any capriciousness on God's part. Quite the contrary. It conveys His desire for an intimate relationship with us.

If, for example, I like worshiping God loudly all the time and feel that the only way I can encounter God is through demonstrative and boisterous worship, then I am making *my* desires the primary measure of worship. And if I fail to cultivate a rich, multilayered understanding of God's character that translates into an equally rich, multilayered worship expression, this could reflect a rather shallow relationship with God.

Imagine for a moment what would happen if I approached my wife, Nancy, the way we often approach God. Having established a certain set of responses with which I feel comfortable, I convey my affection to Nancy the same way—and often at the same time—to the point of robotic repetition. Say I come to

Nancy at seven-thirty in the morning while she's in the kitchen, peck her on the cheek, and say, "Honey, I love you." The second morning, I do the same thing. Then the same on the third morning, the fourth, and so on. Pretty soon she would turn to me and say, "Knock it off! I'm a person!"

What Nancy would be telling me is that because she is a person, she wants me to discern her desires—the way in which she would like me to express affection—and approach her accordingly. For example, there are times when my wife likes me to nestle up close to her while we watch a classic black-and-white movie, and there are times she likes the tiger in me to come out. The variety of ways I can show her my love—and the sensitivity to know which expressions are appropriate at which times—underscores the maturity with which I approach our relationship.

God is a person, and there are times when He wants me to be quiet before Him and times when He wants me to celebrate before Him.

Richard Foster defuses the argument that our predispositions ought to shape our worship:

> We are quick to object to this line of teaching. "People have different temperaments," we argue. "That may appeal to emotional types, but I'm naturally quiet and reserved. It isn't the kind of worship that would meet my needs." What we must see is that the real question in worship is not "What will meet my need?" The real question is "What kind of worship does God call for?"[4]

Quieting our hearts and sensitizing our minds to the Holy Spirit makes us receptive to His promptings, for example, singing softly at one time, but singing triumphantly at another. Some of us come from "high" church backgrounds that prize quiet reflection and studied liturgy. Others of us come from more charismatic backgrounds—give us the closest chandelier and we'll be swinging till Jesus comes. The truth is that worship is both of these and everything in between. We must learn how to worship God the way He wants to receive it.

CENTERED IN THE INNER COURT

Intimacy with and passion for God is nurtured in only one place. Brother Lawrence knew that place. It is a place of such exquisite joy and intoxicating sweetness that he called it "the bosom of God."

Today, knowledge and awareness are increasing exponentially, and we seem to have a rabid compulsion to keep up. We used to laugh about those who tried to keep up with the Joneses—now all of us are trying to keep up with the world. The young need to be hip and the old need to stay relevant. The investor needs to stay ahead of the market and the parent needs to stay ahead of his kids. The pastor must stay abreast of shifting demographics and the politician must keep his eye on shifting poll numbers. Madison Avenue, Wall Street, and Hollywood Boulevard have promised but failed to take us to Easy Street. Silicon Valley hasn't given us peace in our valleys.

The crazier it gets, the more we need to crave His courts. We are *centered* in the inner court. The most relevant people in the future will be those who know the ancient wisdom. The ones who will have the ear of the next generation are the ones whose ears can hear His voice. The more the world changes, the more God stays the same. Those who know Him will be highways of holiness and pathways of peace for the myriad that will soon look for a spring in this twenty-first-century desert.

CHAPTER 4

The Heart of a Bride

I ask you, Lord Jesus, to develop in me, your lover,
an immeasurable urge towards you,
an affection that is unbounded,
a longing that is unrestrained,
a fervor that throws discretion to the winds!

RICHARD ROLLE

W orship is not an end in itself. It is meant to take us somewhere. Worship sensitizes us to God's presence. But even then He wants us to know the security of His presence for an even deeper purpose: *intimacy* with Him. As important as worship is, it is but a pathway to communion with God, the means by which we tether our hearts to His. Our call to worship has *nothing* to do with giving us an opportunity for some cathartic release—it has *everything* to do with elating God's heart by expressing our hunger for Him.

Worship is about intimacy with the Father and His Son, Jesus, about nestling in His everlasting arms, about being romanced by the Ultimate Lover, about bringing joy to the One whose heart absorbs the sting of rejection every second of every day.

It is about being His bride....

Discovering Intimacy with Jesus

I had been a youth pastor for almost a year. Our little midweek group started the school year with around twenty-five people. By the end of that year we had "grown" to a whopping fourteen! I was ready to resign my position and sell shoes, pump gas, mow lawns—anything but subject myself to the disappointment of a ministry in which I was getting little response.

I had tried every trick and gimmick I knew to connect with those young people. I read the manuals, used the lingo, and partied hearty. I packaged the gospel as relevantly as I knew how and generally tried my best to be cool. And for what? A bunch of uninterested kids who sat in the youth service week after week bored stiff. All I was getting from this ordeal was more and more miffed at these could-care-less kids and more convinced that I couldn't succeed at much because I was a jerk, would always be a jerk, and would live the rest of my life wallowing in my mediocrity.

I was desperate and was faced with a decision: Either we were going to see a breakthrough, or I was going to hang it up and leave this youth ministry thing to those who were hipper than I.

On that sunny May day in California, most students were preoccupied with getting out of school and celebrating summer. But while young minds were racing with thoughts of summer fun, I was dreading yet another rousing youth meeting in which I was supposed to once again train my little seals to clap for God.

I was not relishing this one bit, so I sat down and decided

to do something different. I resolved to get there fifteen minutes early, sit down at the piano, and do something I had not done: worship for as long as I wanted. Right in front of the kids! Not to impress them, not to manipulate them, not to force a response. Just to worship Jesus because I wanted to. *After all,* I reasoned, *what have I got to lose? Nothing else is working anyway.*

So I did it. I sat at the piano, closed my eyes, and began to sing—while a handful of teens sat in the room looking at me, puzzled. I worshiped and worshiped, never opening my eyes but just concentrating on Jesus. I had resolved to worship Jesus whether they joined me or not. It was an all-or-nothing moment.

A half hour passed, and several more young people had come into the room. I'm sure they must have wondered what planet I had just come from. But I didn't care. This was not about them or about me. It was not about anything but Jesus.

By now a good twenty kids had shown up, but I just kept worshiping. After about forty-five minutes, I finally looked up and saw almost every one of these kids singing their hearts out, tears streaming down their faces. They were worshiping God, caught up in simply adoring Him.

That was the beginning. For the next nine years, we witnessed astounding growth and worldwide impact. But it all flowed from that one night in which we learned that immersing ourselves in God's presence is priority, that intimacy with God is everything. We discovered firsthand why Moses said, "Unless Your Presence go with us, we are not going" (see Exodus 33:15).

It wasn't long before we found ourselves with scores of young people whose hearts had been kindled with a fire of

desire to know God. At this point I figured I needed to start laying some foundations in their lives. They needed to establish
themselves in the Word so that their newfound zeal wouldn't
wane because of the absence of biblical truth. But what was I to
teach? The Gospel of Mark? I knew that a lot of discipleship
courses began with this book. Or maybe the book of Acts—fire
'em up with visions of the early church. Or perhaps the life of
David, a young man whose passion for God could most certainly provide a tangible model for their own lives.

As I prayed, I distinctly felt that I was to do a verse-by-verse
study of the Song of Solomon. With high schoolers no less! It
flew in the face of convention. It crossed the grain of every
known method of effective youth ministry. It made no sense.
Would high school kids actually get it? Or would they be too
absorbed in the sexual imagery of the book and snicker away
our meeting times?

But something in me reasoned that if these young people
could just fall in love with Jesus, everything else in their lives
would fall into place. So for well over two years I taught them
the story of the King's love for the maiden and her journey to an
intimate place with the Lord. Naturally, we had little difficulty
maintaining a robust attendance.

I'm not suggesting that any other youth pastor should do
this. In fact, as I look back it seems a strange book from which
to launch a discipleship course with a bunch of impressionable
youth. After all, we have them for only a short period of time,
so surely they need to understand Romans or Ephesians, or
learn how to defend their faith, or how to pray. And yet unless

a heart is aflame with an unquenchable love for Jesus, it cannot absorb spiritual truth.

CULTIVATING INTIMACY

The idea of cultivating intimacy with the Lord may strike some as a little irregular. Such language seems to fit more in a dimestore novel than it does in reference to the transcendent Lord of Glory. It seems too common, perhaps too irreverent, or just too chummy—as if our relationship with Him could be reduced to cozy images of a bride nestling up to her bridegroom's breast. But I suggest that the picture of the church as Christ's bride is the sum total of all other biblical metaphors for the people of God.

The theme of bridehood is not incidental in Scripture. It resounds not just in the poetic nuances of Solomon, but through the messages of Hosea, Ezekiel, and Jeremiah. It is demonstrated in the actions of David as he celebrated with abandon before the Lord. And, interestingly enough, it is the last dominant image the Word renders of our relationship with Jesus. In Revelation 21, John is shown the bride, the wife of the Lamb. The description of her perfection and the brilliance with which she shines is awesome and arresting.

Of course, Scripture gives us many pictures and metaphors to describe the church's relationship with God. We are the body of Christ, His temple, the army of the Lord, and the flock of His pasture. Each one of these, of course, is enriching and corresponds with specific aspects of both our relationship with God and our function in the world. That the biblical record ends with the bridal motif suggests that this image captures the very essence of what God is doing in His people. In truth, the picture of the church as the bride of the Bridegroom represents the sum total of all the other metaphors. It is the ultimate consummation of who we are to be in Christ.

This is not to say that the "church as bride" theme means our posture should be one of docility. Quite the opposite. It is a misconception to say that the image of a bride is delicate and thus does not convey a sense of determined militancy. On the contrary, I suggest that the greatest and most militant force the world has ever seen is that of a committed wife defending her husband.

Cultivating a heart for Jesus like that of a bride for her bridegroom radically shapes our motives—the ministries we launch, the priorities we set. Our lives can be motivated out of fear or anger, and both can masquerade as competitiveness or drivenness. But a bride responds not out of fear or anger, nor even a sense of need, but rather out of love for her bridegroom.

Bridal intimacy is cultivated in worship. For our worship is not prepared liturgy alone, nor is it an incidental exercise designed to set the stage for a preacher's sermon. It is a moment of holy embrace. When we lift our hands, we receive His embrace. When we close our eyes in worship, it's like that moment just before two lovers kiss. When we hear the Scriptures preached or nourish our souls as we meditate on its precepts, it's as if the very seed of His Word impregnates our hearts.

I know it's tough for men to buy into such romantic imagery, especially when it calls us to think of ourselves in feminine terms. But heavenly romance is the polar opposite of the tawdry trash served up by Hollywood. Genuine bridal devotion to Jesus suggests a strength of conviction, a durable commitment to sacrifice, and a steadfast grit in the face of adversity that comes only from the heart's fount of love. It is a "muscular" devotion to the Lord that does not demur when its will is crossed by the Bridegroom's commands and is quick to contend for His glory.

A Picture of the Bride

Nowhere in Scripture is our relationship with Jesus as Bridegroom more eloquently and artistically expressed than in the Song of Solomon. The love song between the king and the maiden, while a simple love song in its own right, is nevertheless a true picture of the desire God has for us.[1] The Trinity's full passion finds its singular expression in the Son, Christ Jesus, who courts us, woos us, and draws us to Himself. And when we are drawn to Him, the drivenness that so wearies the soul is muted—and we find solace and satisfaction in His embrace.

Listen to the language of love!

"Let him kiss me with the kisses of his mouth" (1:2).

The maiden's cry shows that she knows her King is not a condescending ruler who benevolently nods from a far-off throne, nor just a gentleman who might politely brush her cheek, but a lover who has more affection for her than can be put into words. She knows him to be a King who desires, in the words of Rabbi Gershom, to hold her so passionately to himself that as "they kiss each other with their mouths it were as if they were attached by their breath which they inhale from the other."[2]

This is the boundless affection, the electric desire, Christ has for you and me. An embrace from the King is not a quick hug and then down to business. He doesn't want us simply to use us, for love casts personal agendas to the wind. He wants us because *He wants us.*

"Draw me...into [your] chambers!" (1:4, KJV).

The maiden abandons all protocol and ignores what others may think of her passion. For she knows that romance is not calculated strategy, but effervescence of desire. As much as she wants him, she knows that it will be more fulfilling to allow the King to set the tone for their love than to impose her own ideas or to attempt to define the relationship her own way. She doesn't demand but rather seeks to be drawn, for by being drawn she will enjoy a deeper level of the King's desire.

Her Beloved is not an option to her—He is life itself. "Draw me!" she cries. If she must wait, then she will wait for His invitation. For the heart that learns to wait on the Lord is a heart that learns to focus on Him. Thus she gives her Lover-King complete freedom to woo her on His terms. She knows that to initiate the relationship for her own security's sake would be to adulterate the depth of intimacy they would enjoy later. She wants to be drawn and to be utterly dependent on Him, which means allowing the King to reveal Himself in the ways and at the pace He chooses. Yet she is not impatient; she waits on Him.

She knows that in the waiting she will see more of Him, and that the more she sees Him the more she is fulfilled. She knows the greater her dependency on Him, the deeper her intimacy with Him. Andrew Murray knew this was the secret to happiness as well: "Never forget [these] two truths," he said. "Your absolute helplessness and God's absolute sufficiency."[3]

"Show me your face, let me hear your voice; for your voice is sweet, and your face is lovely" (2:14).

Here, it is the Bridegroom's turn to express longing for His beloved. To think that the King of the Universe finds our hearts alluring and the sound of our voices pleasurable! This boundless love of Christ is masterfully captured by C. S. Lewis when he says that His love is

> ...not the senile benevolence that drowsily wishes you to be happy in your own way, not the cold philanthropy of a conscientious magistrate, nor the care of a host who feels responsible for the comfort of his guests, but the consuming fire Himself, the Love that made the worlds, persistent as the artist's love for his work and despotic as a man's love for a dog, provident and venerable as a father's love for a child, jealous, inexorable, exacting as love between the sexes.[4]

Later in the story, the bride expresses an inconsolable ache when she can no longer sense His presence.

"If you find my beloved...tell him...I am lovesick" (5:8, NASB).

Sick with love! The gnawing emptiness in the heart that so wants to immerse itself in the object of its affection, that craves its Lover's embrace—but that has lost its way. The Franciscan poet Jacopone of Todi captures this ache:

Mounting in me, like the sun at morn,
    Love breaks my heart, even as a broken blade;
Christ, first and only Fair, from me has shorn
    My will, my wits, and all that in me stayed
I in his arms am laid,
    I cry and call—
"O You my All, O let me die of love!"[5]

Is this our response when we cannot hear Him, when we no longer sense the sweet breath of His Spirit caressing our souls? Do we ache for Him? Are we sick with love?

Worship is as much an expression of lovesickness as it is the awe of His majesty. And sometimes God allows us to walk through the dark corridors of life where we have no answers and do not sense His care. Sometimes the path to realizing the depth of His passion takes us through the valley of the shadow. Somehow, though we don't always see it during those dark nights of the soul, God does a deep, hidden work in us, bringing us into a kind of intimate knowledge of Himself.

Those times when questions loom large and answers are hollow produce a depth of understanding that can be cultivated no other way. John of the Cross tells us why:

Ignorant would he be if he went after God in search of…sweetness, and rejoiced and rested in it; for in this case he would not be seeking God with his will grounded in the emptiness of faith and love, but spiritual sweetness and pleasure, which is of creature, following his taste in desires. Thus he would not love

God purely, above all things…those who are on the right path will set their eyes on God and not on these outward things nor on their inner experiences…they will have all the pleasure taken away so that the soul may be purified. For a soul will never grow until it is able to let go of the tight grasp it has on God.[6]

You see, we can think we're grasping for God when all we're doing is grasping for His blessings. That is why His Holy Spirit is at work in us creating the heart of a bride. For though a bride may endure pain beyond her comprehension, she will not accuse the Lord of injustice or praise Him with reservation. At the point of her deepest despair, she will clutch Jesus in the depths of her heart. She will not love her Bridegroom on her own terms. Her agenda is His glory and nothing else.

The dark times for her are merely chances to hold Him closer. Her moments of blindness are an opportunity to see Him by faith and know an intimacy that reason alone fails to nurture. For the blind often hone their other senses in order to compensate for their loss of sight. They can sense and "see" in ways that those of us who are limited by our physical field of sight cannot. When Helen Keller was asked what was worse than blindness, she replied, "To have eyesight but no vision." When we are blind to what we can figure out, when we cannot see logically, we are forced to touch Him, smell Him, and hear Him much more acutely. When we have been stripped of all else, we can know that He is all that satisfies.

Rekindling the passion to worship

Jesus is my God, Jesus is my Spouse, Jesus is my Life,
Jesus is my only Love, Jesus is my All, Jesus is my Everything.
Because of this I am never afraid. I am doing my work with Jesus,
I'm doing it for Jesus, I'm doing to Jesus;
therefore the results are His not mine.

M O T H E R   T E R E S A

A s I roamed the back streets of Calcutta, the sheer immensity of the poverty overwhelmed me. Millions living their lives out of cardboard shacks, thousands racked with disease. But it was here, I knew, that a little woman waged a huge offensive against the ravages of sin.

Mother Teresa was already world renowned when I was there as a twenty-year-old, cutting my teeth in missions. The real secret to her ministry, I learned, was what she and her Sisters of Charity did every morning. Upon arising they would spend two hours simply adoring Jesus. Not interceding for needs, not petitioning God on behalf of their ministry, not perusing an interesting Bible study—*just worshiping Jesus.*

Down through the centuries, the heart of our call has been sounded in psalms and preached from pulpits: Our ultimate ministry is the worship and adoration of God. And today a rediscovery is going on. In a culture where results are praised and achievement prized, we are once again realizing that man's chief end cannot be measured. That state to which our highest and most noble aspirations are being stirred is a life consumed with a passion to worship God.

PASSIONATE WORSHIP

The Latin phrase *Te Deum*, which means "praise be to God," is often used as a title for prayers and songs in church liturgies. But for many of us, *Te Deum* evokes more "tedium" than passion. How can we maintain a lifelong passion for worship? How can we keep its expression as our highest priority and thus keep our eyes fixed on Jesus?

I believe that when we understand some things about worship, we can then begin to infuse real passion into our worship.

Worship becomes passionate when we realize that to worship is to reflect the image of God.

In my book *I Am: The Unveiling of God*, I discuss one of the most difficult mental roadblocks to worship. Why, if He is indeed a God of unselfish love, does God demand our worship? It seems rather egotistical on God's part, doesn't it? For many, there is a deep hidden reservation about this. We know that God is worthy of our worship and that we were created to worship, but this question still nags at us.

This dilemma actually points us to one of the most thrilling truths about God, and it's a truth that, if we fully understand it, will infuse our worship with passion. We know that all good things flow from the character of God Himself. Since the act of worship is a good thing, its expression must somehow be rooted in God's character. And since God is love, His command that we worship Him must flow out of purely unselfish designs. The love of God has existed eternally within the relationship of the Father, Son, and Holy Spirit. A significant aspect of love is the propensity to adore one another. In a real sense adoration has been going on in the Godhead for all eternity.

At creation, God gave our first parents a wonderful gift: He made them in His image, meaning they had the ability to reason, to feel, to choose, to dream. And because God made them—and us—in His image, part of the package was and is the capacity to adore, which is the seed of our need to worship. So God's command that we worship Him springs not from some selfish desire to be eternally stroked, but rather from the recognition that we are made in His image—designed to adore.

God's summons to worship Him springs from pure unselfishness. We are so valuable to Him that He wants us to adore that which is of the highest worth; therefore, His command to worship Him is not rooted in some divine ego, but rather is consistent with His love.

When we understand this, how can we not passionately worship Him with every fiber of our being? Worship is the closest in this life we come to union with our Beloved and to a place where we experience the very love of the Trinity.[1]

Worship becomes passionate when we realize that we are "other-dimensional."

In Ephesians 2:6, Paul the apostle transports us to a plane of understanding that, if we apprehend it, will infuse our worship with passion. He calls us to see ourselves seated with Christ in heavenly places.

For a long time I thought that was simply Paul's way of being poetic, describing in rhapsodic language our authority in Christ. It sounded to me like Paul was so caught up in the wonder of God's future plan that he spoke about our place in Christ as though it were present tense. Surely Paul didn't mean that we are actually seated with Christ in heaven right now! Or did he?

Considering the possibility that we are actually living in heaven right now seems ludicrous. Yet there is something about Paul's statement here that goes beyond mystical experience, beyond poetic description, beyond the mere rush of emotional exuberance. I suggest that Paul is stating the fact that in a very real—though limited—sense we are dwelling in heaven now. That thought might strike some as odd. One might say, "If this is heaven, then I want out!" But I believe our problem with Paul's assertion that we are "seated with Christ in heavenly places" is that we come to it with preconceived ideas of what heaven is and where it is located.

We are used to perceiving heaven in directional terms, as something above us or beyond the clouds. We have a "Jacob's ladder" view of heaven. This raises some interesting questions. For example, if heaven is above us, then what happens when the earth rotates? And if heaven is beyond the universe, then what does that say about the reality of God's omnipresence? I submit that we are not to understand heaven in directional terms, but in dimensional terms. In other words, heaven is another dimension coinciding with this one. This comes as no surprise to physicists who for years have been musing on the possibility of parallel universes.

I believe that if our spiritual eyes could be completely opened during our worship gatherings, we would quite literally find ourselves in heaven's processional. We would see the ranks of the angelic hosts and the myriad of witnesses who have gone before us, all singing God's praises.

When we came to Christ, we became bi-dimensional people, meaning we live in the heavenly while communicating in the earthly. This is not to suggest that the earthly realm is but a shadow of the heavenly—an idea more akin to Plato than Scripture. It is to say that these two realities coexist and we as believers stand at the threshold. For unbelievers, Christians become, in a sense, the doorway through which they can peek into a spiritual reality they have never known.

Some time ago, I led a group of college students in worship. Seated in the back was a young basketball player. I knew him well enough to know that he was not given to wild spiritual experiences. He was a jock, and he lived for sports and good times.

After the evening's gathering, he came up to me with his eyes as big as his face. "You will never believe what I saw," he said as he stared off into space. "As you were leading worship, I saw two very tall angelic beings—so tall that I could not see their faces. And then behind you I saw the very feet of God."

Was this young man beholding a vision? Perhaps. But I think that for a brief moment his eyes had been opened to see where we are actually living. When Paul wrote that "we are seated with Christ," it was and is in the present tense. And the fact that the young man saw God's feet should not strike us as unscriptural.

In Exodus 24 we read how the elders saw the feet of God on Mt. Sinai. That's just one more amazing thing about God. Though He is omnipresent, He is not limited by His omnipresence. He is so incredible that He is not only everywhere, but He can also localize manifestations of Himself at an infinite number of places simultaneously. So my friend was simply receiving a glimpse of where we live.

When I realize that as I gather with the saints to worship God or I huddle close to my Father's lap in my private times of communion I am quite literally entering the very processional of heavenly worship, how can I worship with my hands in my pockets? How can I worship with my mind a million miles away? No, worship demands the fullest expression of my being.

Worship becomes passionate when we understand that it is the key to experiencing the knowledge of God.
Psalm 22:3 tells us that the Lord inhabits the praises of His people (NKJV). This can also be rendered, "Where God's people praise Him, there He will reveal His presence and authority."[2]

God makes Himself known to a worshiping people, and because He does so, worship becomes more of a privilege than a duty. Though we are *commanded* to praise, it seems we're *allowed* to worship. When we read about worship in heaven in Revelation 4 and 5, the sense we're given is that these heavenly creatures are *allowed* to come near to worship Him.

There is a qualitative difference between praise and worship. Sometimes the words are used interchangeably, but there is a distinction between the two. We might say that praise is a *declaration* of who God is, while worship is an *encounter* with who He is. Praise is the *objective* declaration of His character: "God, You're good. God, You're holy. God, You're glorious." Worship is in part a *subjective* encounter with His character— when we are suddenly caught up in the wonder of His presence and exclaim, "God, You really are all these things!"

Praise stems from an act of the will. I choose to praise Him not because I feel like it but because He is worthy. Worship, on the other hand, has the element of interaction. It is like following the lead of a dance partner—worship is the choreography we enjoy when we respond to each initiative of the Spirit. From another angle, worship is our participation in the Holy Spirit's declaration of the wonders of the Father and the Son.

Why make the distinction? Because if we don't, we may run the risk of treating our worship expression as something we control. If worship is merely a matter of our choice—something we can turn on and off like a light switch—its value is diminished. But if we recognize that when God draws us into His presence we are given this unique *privilege* of echoing His greatness in return, then we will treasure worship.

At the risk of sounding too subjective, I suggest that our worship before the Lord is an interchange between God and His people whereby God leads us ever deeper into the warmth of His embrace. There is a romantic element to it.

Most of us remember our teenage dating experiences. Such

memories may feel delightful or odious to you, but nonetheless some intriguing parallels can be drawn between this romantic interplay and our worship.

You recall the routine—lonely, insecure, pimple-faced boy dies a thousand deaths as he tries to muster the courage to ask lonely, insecure girl out on a date. She has to wait till the guy pops the question, but he delays for fear of rejection. Finally he asks her out, she says yes, and his sense of manhood skyrockets.

They hit it off on the first date, and by the third date he is thinking to himself that he would like to express some "godly affection" to this girl of his dreams (at least his dreams at that moment). So he initiates some appropriate ways he can cozy up to her during their date. He casually stretches out his hand, and if she takes it on her own, it's two points, three if she gives it a squeeze. A little later he puts his arm around her waist as they walk together. If she doesn't pull away, that's a good sign, and if she actually nestles a little closer, it's heaven.

Throughout the evening, these little interchanges of initiation and response continue until the evening finally climaxes with the good-night kiss. It's all been moving toward this moment. So he walks her to the door, looks into her big brown eyes, and as his lips are about to meet hers, her mother comes to the door.

We've all been there. At least, we all used to be there. I'm not advocating certain dating behaviors, but simply drawing an analogy to the kind of thing that happens when we worship God: He initiates and we respond. He reveals a little of Himself, reminds us of His peace, touches our hearts, brings to our minds a timely Scripture. He reveals His nearness to us in these ways, which provokes our praise. God then reveals a bit more of Himself to us, which inspires even more praise. And this divine interchange crescendos to a place where we sense the embrace of His presence.

The angels know this. As I wrote in *I Am:*

> These creatures are permanently caught in a transfiguration, utterly mesmerized by the One they worship. For time beyond time they have been worshiping God with no apparent care for their own existence, enraptured in the pull of divine fascination.... Each time these creatures cry "Holy," God is moved to reveal a facet of His character they have never seen...which causes them to cry "Holy" all the more—which moves God to reveal that much more of Himself. And this has been going on for millennia.[3]

Of course, we don't worship in order to manufacture an experience. Nor is worship the elusive search for an emotional connection to the divine. We simply worship by faith, whether or not we feel anything. There is always the danger of worshiping worship, or making the spiritual experience more important than the God we worship. Such a practice invariably leads not only to deception, but also to a distorted view of grace. Taken to its logical conclusion, such an approach would lead the worshiper to believe that if he doesn't achieve some ecstatic experience, either he has not worshiped effectively or God is displeased with him.

On the other hand, to swing in the direction of disconnecting worship from genuine experience is to invite a coldness of heart, the deterioration of praise and worship into mere form and ritual without the passion for genuine encounters with our Father. Though we live in a romanticized world where feelings seem to determine value, we mustn't become so suspicious of emotion that we're afraid to cultivate the spiritual sensitivities of discernment, reflection, and the ability to receive spiritual insight from Scripture.

In ancient times on the day of *Yom Kippur* (the Day of Atonement), when the high priest entered the inner court, he stood in front of the veil separating the Holy Place from the Most Holy Place in which the ark of the covenant was placed. That veil was thick and without seam. It was not a curtain that could be drawn to allow the priest to enter casually. The latter temple actually had two curtains separated by a couple of feet, which provided a kind of corridor through which the priest would have to walk. He entered one side and had to walk the length of the curtain before passing through the second veil. This suggests the incredible caution—the fear of the Lord, if you will—with which the High Priest came into God's presence.

A. W. Tozer once wrote:

> Worship rises or falls with our concept of God; that is
> why I do not believe in these half conceited cowboys
> who call God the man upstairs. I do not think they
> worship at all because their concept is unworthy of God
> and unworthy of them. And if there is one terrible disease in the church of Christ, it is that we don't seek God
> as great as He is. We are too familiar with God.[4]

The only way to truly enter in to God's presence is through abject humility—a heart that is prostrate before Him in reverence. Though He is always with us, our sensitivity to His presence is in large part determined by our obedience to Him and our understanding of His ways.

Cyril of Jerusalem, one of the great early church fathers, put it this way:

> Remission of sins is equally given to everyone; communion with the Holy Ghost is given in proportion to each person's faith. If you have worked little, you receive little. But if you have worked hard, the reward is great. Cleanse your vessel so that you can receive grace more abundantly.[5]

Worship becomes passionate when we understand that worship is a reenactment of the Resurrection.

The dedication of Solomon's temple was one of the most incredible displays of God's glory recorded in Scripture. Upon completion of the temple, Solomon prayed, "Now arise, O LORD God, and come to your resting place" (2 Chronicles 6:41). In response to his prayer, God revealed His glory so mightily that the priests had to scurry out of the temple.

We can draw parallels between that temple and the temple Peter says is formed with the hearts of those who love Jesus (1 Peter 2:5, 9–10). This is a temple made not of brick or wood, but of human lives. And just as He demonstrated His glory in the old temple, so He desires to demonstrate His glory in the new temple.

In Solomon's prayer, "Come and rise to your rest," we get a

sense that we can pray the same thing: "Come, Lord Jesus, and rise within Your people!" Herein is a striking parallel. I suggest that something about the rising of the glory of the Lord in Solomon's temple speaks of the dynamic that happens in the act of worship. Could it be that the power of Jesus "rises" in our midst when we worship? Going a bit further, can we not see in the act of worship a certain *reenactment* of the Resurrection?

Consider: The same power that raised Christ from the dead begins to rise within a body of believers that worships in spirit and in truth. This dynamic is so palpable that it becomes something of a participation in His resurrection life. We know that according to the Scriptures, Christ died and rose again once and for all and is presently seated at the right hand of the Father. But just as the Eucharist—the Lord's Supper—speaks to the remembrance of Christ's crucifixion, so the act of worship speaks to the celebration of His resurrection.

Perhaps we should view worship sacramentally. For regardless of how we view the sacraments, one thing we can agree on: A sacrament is not empty ritual, but something we treat with the utmost reverence because it is an expression of God's presence. Thus when we partake of the Lord's Table, we know that a spiritual interaction takes place between us and God. It's as if God reserves a unique expression of His presence just for those times when we eat the bread and drink the cup.

We would not think of taking the bread and cup irreverently. Yet if during our corporate gatherings we worship with unfocused minds—wishing the preacher would cut to the sermon so we can get through the service and on to our own agendas—wouldn't it seem pretty careless? If we saw worship as sacrament, I don't think we would come with our mind a million miles away, wondering if our team won the championship or if we should sell some stock. Rather, we would come before the Lord with intense focus, treasuring every moment in His presence.

Just as there is a unique expression of His presence when His Word is preached, so there is a unique manifestation of the Lord's presence that occurs when we worship. For in preaching, the Holy Spirit takes God's Word and makes it life to the hearer. Likewise, when we sincerely worship the Lord, we sensitize our hearts to His presence. And as moment by sweet moment passes, it's as if His presence becomes magnified. Our sense of who He is increases as we tune out the dissonance of the world and tune in to Him.

The apostle Paul wrote, "Be filled with the Spirit, speaking to one another in psalms and hymns and spiritual songs, singing and making melody with your heart to the Lord" (Ephesians 5:18–19, NASB). The word *filled* in this context suggests our ever-present *need* to be filled. It implies the necessity to stay under the Spirit's control and our constant need to subject our "self-bent" to His mastery. This process of coming under His control—and the Spirit taking control—can be captured in the sense of our increased awareness of His nearness, or His "rising up" within us.

Paul establishes a definite connection between the rising up of the Spirit in our hearts and our obedience in worshiping and praising Him. Thus the parallel: As Jesus rose from the dead in power and is now seated at the Father's right hand, so His Holy Spirit rises up within us in power. It is a way in which we taste of His resurrection life. It is a way, in a sense, that the Resurrection event echoes to the present day.

If worship distinctly serves to remind us of the wonder of Christ's resurrection, how can we worship halfheartedly? And though we should never worship to capture a feeling, we can nevertheless trust the Lord that as we worship, we will more intensely sense His presence.

It is said that one night as Francis of Assisi was in prayer he was suddenly caught up in an encounter with the awesome majesty of God. Like a man whose very breath had been sucked out of him, he lay there, prostrate before Him. Words failed him. All that would come to him was "My God! My God! What art Thou? And what am I?" Far from intimidating him, this revelation of God's glory and majesty caused Francis to forever throw himself into the arms of the One who, though so grand and powerful, deigned to unveil Himself before mere creatures of dust.

Perhaps that which infuses our worship with passion more than anything else is the very revelation of God.

Worship was never meant to be a slot in our lives, nor a mere addendum to a frenetic schedule, nor an add-on to ministry. Worship is the core of our responsiveness to God. The expression of worship keeps our hearts receptive to grace, opens our minds to allow the Holy Spirit to illumine Scripture, motivates us to persevere in prayer, and consistently sensitizes us to the needs of others.

Worship is the headwater of all other ministry flow. No wonder Mother Teresa spent so much time simply adoring Jesus. Though at times she must have felt like an island in a sea

of need and misery, she knew that to touch anyone else effectively she had to first touch God in that place of simple contemplation.

So many wander through life looking for personal meaning,
trying to discern their destiny. The worship of God is the end of
the search, for it turns our *wander* into *wonder.*

CHAPTER 6

Renewing our minds through worship

*More life may trickle out of a man through thought
than through a gaping wound.*

THOMAS HARDY

Recently a young man asked me to summarize in one
sentence the essence of the Christian life. I raced
through my mental files of principles and attitudes that could
give him the bottom line he was looking for: worship, grace,
humility.

How does one reduce the sublime to one sentence?

Then a Scripture came to me: "Enoch walked with God"
(Genesis 5:24). That's it! That's life! Simply walking with God!
Not merely having appointments with Him or just serving Him.
Not racing to fulfill a mission or juggling a dozen priorities with
the finesse of an acrobat, but just walking in a moment-by-
moment communion with our Beloved.

That seemed to sum it all up. And by the look of satisfaction on that young man's face, I could tell that by the grace of
God I had hit the mark.

Communion with God is the joy of life. There simply is no
other lasting satisfaction. In His embrace, all of life becomes an

encounter with Him; every day is charted by the whispers of His voice; every moment becomes a potential quiet time.

But many of us don't have quiet minds. They churn with apprehensions. Like an ocean roiling in a hurricane, waves of fear crest and crash in our minds—memories of put-downs and brush-offs, the chorus of coaches, companions, and competitors we feel we have to please and answer to. Our thoughts are often held hostage by these emotional predators, our inner life and fire drained—for we are prisoners of our memories.

But our Father in heaven promises to renew our minds, heal our hearts, and free us from the inner strongholds, which my friend Dan Sneed defines as "negative thought patterns that are so strongly etched on our minds, they govern our entire thinking process."[1] All we need to do is make ourselves available to the artistry and ministry of His Holy Spirit.

Our inner-court ministry to God creates an atmosphere of warm communion. It starts with worship, but there are other spiritual disciplines that enrich our relationship with Him. As we continue to mine the imagery of Ezekiel 44, let's focus on three aspects of our personal devotional life that can enlarge our capacity for intimacy: the renewal of the mind, biblical meditation, and prayer.

RENEWING THE MIND: PUTTING ON THE LINEN TURBAN

The priest not only clothed himself with linen; he also placed on his head a linen turban (Ezekiel 44:18). One application here relates to Paul's call to be transformed by the renewing of our

minds (Romans 12:2). The renewal of our minds is no periph-
eral issue or optional discipline. In fact, when Paul begins the
practical theology section of his letter to the Romans (chapters
12–16), he lays this essential foundation: "Offer your bodies as
living sacrifices…this is your spiritual act of worship. Do not
conform any longer to the pattern of this world, but be transformed by the renewing of your mind" (12:1–2).

This is what I call prespiritual spirituality. It is the stuff that
has to occur before we can till the soil of obedience and humility. When it comes to spirituality, we often focus on changing
our behavior. If we could just pray more, read the Bible more,
watch our tongue more, share our faith more, guard our eyes
better, and so forth. Yet so many believers become frustrated at
precisely this point. They try to be obedient, fail, and become
discouraged. And this cycle sucks them into a whirlpool of
despair, robbing them of their passion for God.

This despair is rooted not only in our substandard spiritual
performance, but also in a much more basic psychological
dynamic to which Dallas Willard refers: "It is human nature to
resist deep inward change, for such change threatens our sense
of personal identity." Willard goes on to quote theologian Alister
McGrath as he prods us to take seriously the Christlikeness to
which we are intended to conform. "Leading writers now
acknowledge that 'God wishes His people to possess…the fullness of life' that Christian spirituality recognizes in Jesus. What
a stunning thought.… Somehow the seriously thought-out
intention to actually bring about the fullness of life in Christ
must be reestablished."[2]

Of course, the process of being conformed into His likeness

is not a matter of sheer willpower but of positioning ourselves to allow the Holy Spirit to accomplish that work in us. That is why in the first couple of verses in Romans 12, Paul wisely summons us to Christlikeness with a fourfold plan.

Present yourselves a living sacrifice.

The enemy has greatly twisted and distorted the word *sacrifice*. The image of a little lamb lying helplessly on the altar moments before its throat is slit and the blood drained from its woolly body does not evoke feelings of comfort, security, or happiness.

Sacrifice suggests an image of not being in control, of utter resignation and helplessness, of impending death. Yet our glorious destiny is to be a living sacrifice. The Holy Spirit chooses this image for Paul because He wants to convey to us the completeness of our freedom. And freedom is precisely the point. He doesn't want us to be in control, and He is not asking us to take responsibility. He is not calling us to be dynamic initiators. He is saying, "Celebrate your helplessness and revel in your absolute dependence."

Hannah Whitall Smith addressed this in her book *The Christian's Secret of a Happy Life*:

> Let the ways of childish confidence and freedom from
> care, which so please you and win your hearts in your
> own little ones, teach you what should be your ways
> with God; and, leaving yourselves in His hands, learn
> to be literally "careful for nothing"; and you shall
> find…that the peace of God shall garrison your hearts
> and minds through Christ Jesus.[3]

The heart of the one who resolves to be a living sacrifice is one not of passive resignation, but of dynamic disengagement. For example, when we analyze political infighting or struggles for dominance, we often speak of someone "staying above the fray"—the politician strategically remains emotionally detached and uninvolved in the struggle. He does so because he needs to keep his moral bearings in order to respond wisely to situations as they unfold. To become enmeshed in the struggle would disqualify him from speaking to both parties, conciliating, and making peace.

Dynamic detachment is not withdrawal from social intercourse or adoption of an uncaring attitude or succumbing to fatalism. It is recognition of God's sovereignty and our complete dependence on Him, which we express by our absolute trust that He is in control in everything. It is not "dropping out" but "centering on."

A reasonable act of worship.

Living out our lives as living sacrifices—as dependent, trusting, accepting people—is reasonable not only for us, but also for our world. The attitude of dependence makes for cooperative people who aren't driven by personal agendas and aren't fighting over rights. A truly dependent person is a truly strong person. It is only reasonable to adopt this posture of living sacrifice, and it is the only legitimate posture of a worshipful heart.

Do not be conformed to this world.

Here's where we often lose our skirmishes with the enemy. Because we live in a society that has fostered the need for instant gratification, we fail to appreciate the process of thoroughly cleansing toxins from our spiritual bloodstream.

I recently binged over the holidays—chocolate bonbons, peanut butter fudge, eggnog, Russian tea cake, cookies, pecan pie—and I was, of course, feeling lethargic and miserable. So I picked up a box of cleansing tea. The directions said that if I drank this tea over a period of several weeks, modified my diet, and fasted, my body would be cleansed of the toxins that had built up through my bad eating habits.

It wasn't the tea that bothered me so much as the tedious and lengthy process the directions outlined. I was dismayed. It had taken only a few days to pig out, and I was looking for a fix to my physiology that was just as quick. But I had to recognize that my body was telling me that all was not well. It was going to take a slow, focused process not only to shed a few pounds, but also to cleanse my system from the impurities that had built up over a period of time.

Just as poor eating habits can compromise our health, unquestioned thought patterns can suffocate our spirits. We have grown up in a system of thinking shaped by self-interest, pride, fear, and jealousy, and these thought patterns can become deeply ingrained in our minds. To counter these destructive mental habits, we must analyze how these worldly thought patterns continue to shape our minds, identify the "entry points," and learn the tactics of countering their effect. We need to find ways to manufacture fat-free potato chips for our minds so that what we are exposed to in this world passes through our spiritual system without being absorbed. And we do this through the process of renewing our minds.

Be transformed by the renewing of your minds.

The word *mind* here is the Greek word for *intellect*. It is that part of our mind that processes and filters information. It is here that thinking patterns are set. Paul is saying that how we think and how we evaluate information must be changed from a worldly pattern to a godly one. Yet a renewal of thought patterns is the result of the Holy Spirit acting upon *another* part of our mind.

When Jesus said, "You shall love the Lord your God with all your heart, soul, mind and strength" (Mark 12:30), He was not using the same word for *mind* as Paul used in Romans 12:2. It is not the word for *intellect* but for *imagination*. It is in this sphere of our thinking that our minds are renewed. Our intellect receives and evaluates information while our imagination illustrates that information. Jesus is saying that we ought to love the Lord our God with our imagination. How do we do that? One way is to allow the Holy Spirit to paint images of truth on the canvas of our minds.

When Paul exhorts us, "Let this mind be in you which was also in Christ Jesus" (Philippians 2:5, NKJV), the text in the Greek suggests our active mental participation in conforming to the image of Christ's humility as described in the hymn that follows (vv. 6–11). In other words, we are to exercise our minds according to Christ's pattern.

In Isaiah 26:3 we read: "You will keep him in perfect peace, whose mind is stayed on You" (NKJV). The word in the Hebrew for *mind* means "to act as a gatekeeper." Again, this points to the imagination. We have a choice as to what we entertain on the picture screen of our mind. And it is what we allow on that screen that forms the thought patterns that determine behavior.

If we constantly see ourselves blowing up at rude drivers, for instance, we will spawn hotheaded behaviors that will affect other relationships.

Commenting on the centrality of the imagination to the process of biblical meditation (to which we shall shortly turn), Richard Foster says, "The inner world of meditation is most easily entered through the door of the imagination. We fail today to appreciate its tremendous power. The imagination is stronger than conceptual thought and stronger than the will. In the West, our tendency to deify the merits of rationalism—and it does have merit—has caused us to ignore the value of the imagination."[4]

So how does exercising the imagination work practically?

One of my first mission trips as a young adult took me to the big island of Hawaii. Now, I know that doesn't sound like much of a mission trip, but believe me, it was. After a few days at the missions grindstone, I found myself fighting thoughts of inferiority, inadequacy, and failure. I felt like a chicken heart when it came to personal witnessing. As a team leader, I felt incompetent.

As I worshiped the Lord one morning, I began to realize that I could be renewed in my mind in a very practical way. I imagined myself walking with Jesus on a street in the town where I was ministering—Jesus and me hand in hand, reaching out to people, touching them, sharing the Father's love with them. As we walked together, we came to a plaza in the center of town. Turning around, still clasping the hand of Jesus, I saw a crowd of a thousand people. I then saw myself preaching with fervor and excitement, spurred on by the touch of the Master.

In those few moments of worshipful meditation, I had allowed the Holy Spirit to paint in my mind an image of faith that began to replace images of inferiority.

This is a very practical discipline, and we can apply it to any number of areas in our lives. For example, if we are fighting pride, we can picture ourselves in a time of worship washing the feet of someone who rubs us the wrong way. In this way, we replace images of pride and arrogance with images of humility and service. These are not simple mind games or the spin of psychological technique. This is a biblical process. It is learning to love the Lord our God with our imagination, to exercise our mind after the pattern of Christ, and to act as a gatekeeper that allows only those thoughts that reflect the fruits of the Spirit to dominate our thinking patterns.

This process takes time. Replacing thoughts of jealousy, fear, anger, bitterness, pride, and self-sufficiency with thoughts that reflect the fruits of the Spirit doesn't happen overnight. But "putting on the linen turban" is an essential part of our communion with the Lord.

THE BREAD OF HIS PRESENCE: THE PRACTICE OF BIBLICAL MEDITATION

When the priests came into the first room of the inner court, the Holy Place, they passed a table on which lay twelve loaves of bread, symbolizing the twelve tribes of Israel. In Exodus 25:30, this table is called the table of showbread, but the *New American Standard Bible* translates this as "the bread of the Presence," which is much more descriptive. These twelve loaves suggest the fellowship God wants to have with us, specifically that He wants to "sit at table" with us. But it also points to another application: that the Scriptures are not just manuscripts to be studied but words to be branded on our minds by the Holy Spirit's power.

Over the past several years, evangelical believers have begun rediscovering a long-neglected discipline: meditation in the Word. That this discipline has been neglected so long shows both how much we have been co-opted by three centuries of Western rationalism and the deep suspicion we have of anything that smacks of Eastern mysticism. But biblical meditation is fundamentally different. Richard Foster spells out that difference: "Eastern meditation is an attempt to empty the mind; Christian meditation is an attempt to empty the mind in order to fill it. The two ideas are radically different." In fact, the Bible—especially the Psalms—is replete with insights into this essential art.[5]

Meditation is the process whereby the Holy Spirit makes the *written* Word life to us, thus making it the *living* Word, which can then be absorbed into our spiritual systems. Campbell McAlpine defines it this way: "Meditation is the devotional practice of pondering the words of a verse, or verses of Scripture, with a receptive heart, allowing the Holy Spirit to take the written Word and apply it as the Living Word in our inner being."[6]

One of the great Old Testament images on this is Ezekiel 2:9–3:3, in which the Lord holds out a scroll to Ezekiel and tells him to "eat it." That is a great picture of what meditation is all about. It is *eating* the Scriptures.

The call to meditate hits us right from the get-go in Psalm 1:

Blessed is he who meditates in the law day and night, "he shall be like a tree planted by the rivers of water…and whatever he does shall prosper" (vv. 1–3, NKJV). The word *meditation* here in Hebrew is *hagah,* and it means "to mumble, to mutter, to ponder, to make a quiet sound such as sighing." It conveys the state of being so lost in concentration that the one doing the meditating becomes oblivious to everything else around him.

Have you ever seen someone get so lost in thought that his eyes widen as if he is staring off into some distant horizon, transfixed on some image or incident far far away—so much so that he actually begins to mumble to himself, mindless of his surroundings? That is the image being conveyed here: such intense concentration on the Scriptures that no competing thought or agenda can intrude.

From this practice of meditation comes the Jewish custom of *davening,* a special form of prayer in which the supplicant rhythmically rocks back and forth while repeating the Scriptures over and over in his mind.[7] This practice has the effect of focusing the devotee on the Scriptures themselves. It helps him to block out all distraction and allow his mind to concentrate solely on the Word. One important boundary to keep in mind: Biblical meditation does not mean blanking one's mind, but rather focusing one's mind on Scripture.

How does a person achieve this state of concentration? John 1:14 may provide guidance for us: "The Word became flesh and dwelt among us" (NKJV).

This text obviously refers to the incarnation of the Lord Jesus. But it can offer us a useful path to follow as we prepare our minds to meditate in the Scriptures.

The Word

Insight from Scripture is the fuel for our worship. Thus, we must value the Word. Campbell McAlpine hit the mark when he wrote: "Our love [for God] is shown by love for His Word. You cannot separate a person from their voice. If you love a person, you will love their voice, and God's Word is His voice to us."[8]

We must approach God with faith that He wants to make the Word alive to us. Many never get past first base because they don't approach the Word with faith—faith that says, "I know that God wants to reveal insights from the Scriptures even more than I want to receive them. So I come expecting the Word to come alive to me." McAlpine underscores the Lord's desire to make His Word real to us: "There is nothing better we can give to God in worship than that which He Himself inspired."[9]

Became flesh

God's desire is to make the *written* Word the *living* Word. Likening the Scriptures to the essential but external frame of divine revelation, A. W. Tozer writes, "We have forgotten that the essence of spiritual truth cannot come to the one who knows the external shell of truth unless there is first a miraculous operation of the Spirit within the heart."[10]

Again I quote Campbell McAlpine:

Many times a verse, or verses of Scripture, are like flowers that have closed their petals because the sun has gone down. You look at the flower and admire it because it's part of God's creative miracle, but there is much beauty you cannot see. In the morning when the sun rises, the flower begins to open up towards the light, and then you can see the full beauty in colors and details. In the same way we can look at Scripture and know that it is good because God is the author, and yet fail to behold the beauty and detail it contains. However as you meditate, dependent on Divine illumination by the Sun of Righteousness, revelation and insight come, giving you increased knowledge of the Creator.[11]

We can allow the Holy Spirit to take the written Word and make it the living Word by following these simple steps:

1. Put on the linen: Acknowledge His grace; quiet your heart; yield to the Spirit.

2. Look at one verse and break it down into separate phrases. Repeat the first phrase several times slowly. Let the stress of your enunciation fall on different key words in the phrase. For example, take the passage in Habakkuk 2:4, NKJV: "The just shall live by his faith." As you repeat it over and over, say, "The *just* shall live by his faith," then "The just shall *live* by his faith," then "The just shall live by his *faith.*"

3. As you do this, isolate individual words and ask yourself, *What does this mean in the context of the passage?* You will find yourself asking many questions as you focus on the text. *Where does this verse fit in context? Which verses have*

gone before? Which come after? What insights about God does this verse illuminate? What benefits do they describe? What responses are required of me?

And dwelt among us

As we are applying it here, in John 1:14, we can read *among* as *in*. As the Word comes alive to us—that is, as the Holy Spirit draws a connection between the text and our needs according to the grid of our understanding, history, and experience—we need to take further steps to digest the Word. If a passage jumps off the page and the lights go on in our mind—in other words, it makes sense—let's not stop there. Let's use that fresh insight to ignite our worship, praising God for what we've just discovered in the Word. The way that we digest truth is through worship. It is that practice that gets truth from the mind to the heart.

A RENEWED MIND, AN INTIMATE WALK

"Enoch walked with God" (Genesis 5:24).

A communion so close that he did not die a conventional death but simply slipped into the eternal realm he had enjoyed for so long. Finding that stride of fellowship with God transforms all of life. That great fifth-century missionary to Ireland, St. Patrick, knew that stride:

> I see His blood upon the rose
> > And in the stars the glory of His eyes
> His Body gleams amid eternal snows,
> > His tears fall from the skies.

I see His face in every flower
    The thunder and the singing of the birds
Are but His voice—and carved by His power
    Rocks are His hidden words.
All pathways by His feet are worn,
    His strong heart stirs the ever-beating sea,
His crown of thorns is twined with every thorn,
    His cross is every tree.[12]

Historian Paul Johnson best sums it up in his most personal book, *The Quest for God:*

> In the end, that is what the love and worship of God is all about: to turn our minds, and…bodies too, away from the self to goodness, and from the flesh to the spirit. This act of turning we should do every day of our lives…so that in the end it becomes second nature and we cease to need to turn, but become one with [Him] in whom alone we find peace and our destiny.[13]

CHAPTER 7

Breathing in His presence through prayer

It is best to pray briefly, but often.

COTTON MATHER

Prayer. The word conjures conflicting images in our minds. The sweet moment when we sense that God hears us. The guilt we feel for not having prayed. The relief that we have a God to turn to in times of crisis. The weariness of trying to discipline ourselves to stumble out of bed at four-thirty each morning for unproductive quiet times. The thrill of entering into the Father's heart in intercession for the nations. The feeling of being taken to the woodshed because we've faltered in prayer yet again.

We seem to have a love/hate relationship with prayer. We value it, but we usually feel so guilty about our prayer life that we spiritually slouch our way to an apathy that can threaten the health of our souls. Yet as we continue to reflect on the truths of the inner court, we will discover some fresh ways in which we can understand the discipline of prayer.

The Lampstand: Knowing His Presence through Prayer

Situated to the left of the priest as he entered the inner court was a seven-stemmed lampstand. The lampstand symbolizes many truths central to the believer's life: the light of God's glory, the necessity of the Spirit's fresh oil, the light that should shine through God's people to the nations. The individual lamps, which were shaped like almond blossoms, suggest God's care over His people and the fulfillment of His promises.

Seen through the lens of one's individual communion with God, the candlestick can be illustrative of our prayer life, for it conveys the reciprocity and fellowship with God we enjoy in prayer. In prayer we receive the fresh supply of the Spirit and encounter God's light of understanding and direction. And we are reminded of His promises, which become the grounds of our petitions.

Perhaps no other Christian discipline has been written about and discussed—or has been the whipping post of guilt—as much as prayer. We know that prayer is central to a believer's life. In fact, God works primarily through prayer. As E. M. Bounds stated, "God conditions the very life and prosperity of His cause on prayer."[1] William Temple, responding to critics who said that answered prayer was nothing more than coincidence, said, "When I pray, coincidences happen; when I don't, they don't."[2]

Prayer is important to God. In fact, He actively seeks two kinds of people: intercessors and worshipers. Intercession is central to God's strategy. Yet try as we might, many of us still have a tough time engaging in prayer. And the reason may lie in the assumptions we subconsciously bring to its exercise. It may be that we need to adjust how we think about prayer before we will be motivated to pray.

Often we regard prayer as a resource for our ministry or for the responsibilities God has given us. We pray for blessing on our kids and for success in the enterprises we undertake. Yet this approach dilutes the significance of prayer, for we can come to view prayer as a resource *for* ministry rather than as the central drive *of* ministry.

Our mind-set needs some adjusting. It is not a matter of praying *for ministry,* but rather seeing that prayer *is ministry*. If we are being made like Jesus and if His present ministry is that of intercession, prayer should be the bull's-eye of our ministry as well. If we view prayer as the essential fountainhead from which all else flows, instead of just a resource, we will be motivated to pray.

PRAYER: BREATHING IN THE SPIRITUAL REALM

There are many who labor under guilt when it comes to the issue of prayer. But that needn't be the case.

In Luke 18:1–8, Jesus sets forth in a parable some of the most profound insights ever given on prayer. In the story, a widow incessantly harangues an unprincipled judge for legal protection. He stubbornly refuses her entreaties, but soon her persistence wears him down, and he consents to her plea. Her persistence results in her survival.

One of the reasons God so emphasizes prayer is that it is the only way we can survive in the spiritual realm. In the parable, the widow is desperate. If she doesn't procure the judge's protection, her life is in jeopardy.

Jesus told this story to underscore the importance of persevering prayer. But why this emphasis on perseverance? It's not because God doesn't hear us the first time or because He is waiting for us to fulfill a certain quota—as if we earn answers by the amount of prayer we offer. Rather, it is to stress the need to persist in prayer because our lives are at stake.

That's why in verse 8 Jesus connects persistence in prayer to the presence of faith. Faith is the faculty of spiritual sight we begin to recover in our relationship with God. Faith is to the spiritual realm what our eyes are to the physical. Unless we function by faith, the writer of Hebrews says, we cannot please Him (Hebrews 11:6). It is not so much that the absence of faith sends God into a snit. Rather, it is the fact that the very essence of spiritual life cannot work except by faith. Like a tool that doesn't work without batteries, we can't function apart from faith. God isn't displeased by our lack of faith because He is petty, but because without faith we can't connect to His life. And if we can't connect to His life, we die. That is why prayer, which cultivates faith, is not just a good idea; it is essential to our survival.

Jesus' emphasis on persistent prayer doesn't have as much to do with our own determination as with the nature of continuousness itself. Perhaps the intent of the parable in Luke 18 is not simply to prod us to be more determined or more disciplined. I think Jesus was instead pointing to the essential character of prayer by pointing out that, like breathing, it is both natural and essential. Just as faith is *seeing* in the spiritual dimension, prayer is *breathing* in the spiritual dimension.

The call to persistence is not a terse reminder of our spiritual ineptitude but the simple recognition that all of life is meant to be a prayer. When Paul enjoins us to "pray without ceasing" (1 Thessalonians 5:17, NASB), he is not summoning us to scale an impossible height of discipline, reachable by only the spiritual elite. Rather, He is inviting us to view life through spiritual lenses.

To "pray without ceasing," P. T. Forsythe once said, "is far from being absurd because…every man's life is in some sense a continual state of prayer. For what is his life's prayer but its ruling passion? All energies, ambitions, and passion are but expressions of a hunger, a draft, a practical demand upon the future upon the unattained and the unseen."[3] Thus everything can be a point of prayer, thanksgiving, and praise. In fact, carrying this analogy further, worship may be seen as the inhale of breathing, prayer the exhale. We receive from God in worship; we respond to God in intercession.

Richard Lovelace speaks to the burdens some of us in spiritual leadership have placed on people in our attempts to compel them to greater prayer. He maintains that the New Testament evidence indicates that teachings on prayer emphasize short prayers whose "aim is precisely to avoid overloading the conscience of the beginner or the weak believer, to avoid any emphasis on works which will distract us from the recognition of God's grace, and to fix our attention on God who hears and answers, rather than on the mechanism of prayer." Lovelace likens prayer to natural biological processes. "As pain tells us of the need for healing, worry tells us of the need for prayer."[4]

Jesus is trying to get us to see prayer as a reflex, not as an event or slot in our lives. When we understand that prayer is actually a reflex, our every thought can become a point of prayer.

Prayer is to a specific need what the heart is to the body. Just as the heart pumps continuously, sending blood to the organs, prayer sends a constant supply to those for whom we're praying; for in response to prayer, the Holy Spirit graces them with strength, insight, and hope. That is why Paul did not hesitate to credit both the saints' prayers and the Spirit's supply for his effectiveness (Philippians 1:19–20). That is why we are to pray and keep on praying, or to borrow a current acrostic, PUSH—Pray Until Something Happens! This may seem like meaningless repetition, but Jesus didn't negate repetition; He negated *vain* repetition.

There is a spiritual life flow that is dependent on our obedience in prayer. Back to Paul's call to "pray without ceasing": Why such a seemingly impossible command? Because Paul knew that spiritual life is released proportionate to prayer. In light of that, perhaps prayerlessness is more a tragedy than a sin. If we don't breathe, our biological faculties simply shut down and we die. Likewise, without prayer our spirits atrophy.

PRAYER: GETTING TO WHERE GOD IS

Prayer doesn't bring God to us; it takes us to God.

Let me explain. In Hebrews 4 we are told to enter into His rest. We often think of rest as something we are to achieve, as if resolving our inner turmoil results in rest. But we don't come into rest by solving our problems; we come into rest by entering *His* rest.

When we are faced with anger or anxiety—those twin ene-mies of our soul—we tend to view the solution as God coming and fixing us, or at least our problems. For example, we look at a present situation causing us anger or anxiety, and we pray, "God, come and deliver me from my anger," or "God, relieve my anxiety." Generally, those kinds of prayers don't work, and if we continue to pray that way over time, we lose our appetite for prayer.

God is not so much interested in coming to address our anxiety as He is in bringing us into His place of rest. Rather than ask God to solve the problems causing our anxiety, we should see our anxiety as an indication that we are not where God is.

We should wait in God's presence, allowing the Spirit to give us insight into why we're battling anger or anxiety in a par-ticular situation. Let's say I'm angry with an associate with whom I'm partnering on a given project. Rather than pray for God to relieve my anger or fix my partner, I should wait on the Lord and ask Him to show me where *He* is in the whole thing. As I wait in His presence, I can mentally rearrange the bits and pieces of my situation, considering several different scenarios. With each mental image, I wait until I sense His rest.

For example, if I imagine not having partnered with that per-son in the first place and sense His peace at that point, it may indicate that I did not seek God in detail about whom I was to partner with. Perhaps I entered the partnership presumptuously. Since God wasn't in the partnership to begin with, He won't release His peace. Or perhaps, as I keep rearranging the details in my mind, I think back on the moment I did feel peace about partnering with that person. Then perhaps the lack of peace entered because I didn't perceive God's time line in the matter. As I reflect on that as a reason for my anger and suddenly sense His peace, it indicates that God was in the partnership but not in the schedule we set for ourselves.

If we are anxious about something, we can pause to seek God in detail as to what adjustments we are to make. Like a mathematical problem, we can tinker with the numbers until the equation equals rest. This is what I mean when I say prayer doesn't bring God to us; it brings us to God.

Prayer gets us to where God is. Most of the time, the answers we need are not found by fixing the problems, but by seeing where we have strayed from our place of abiding in Jesus.

We see this principle in the prayer Jesus taught us to pray: "Our Father who is in heaven..." Jesus calls us to go where God is. It is instructive to look at the Galatians 5 passage on the fruit of the Spirit as not just that which He produces in us, but that which is essentially the Holy Spirit's nature. In light of that, we might call the fruit of the Spirit the "atmosphere of the Spirit," for wherever the Holy Spirit is, there will be a spiritual environment of love, joy, peace, patience, faithfulness, meekness, gentleness, goodness, and self-control.

PRAYER: LETTING GOD REDEFINE OUR NEEDS

In Luke 10:38–42 we read the account of Christ's visit to Mary and Martha's home. Christ and His disciples show up, sending dear Martha scurrying about to make provisions for her guests. Mary, apparently oblivious to her sister's hard work, sits at Jesus' feet, totally enraptured by His teaching. This unnerves Martha, who complains to Jesus about Mary's insensitivity to the needs at hand. But Jesus mildly chides Martha. "You're bothered by so many things," He tells her. "Your sister has chosen the best thing, and it shall not be taken from her" (see v. 41). Scripture doesn't elaborate, but Martha was no doubt chagrined.

The issue here is not Mary's superspirituality or Martha's superficiality, but rather Christ's right as Lord to redefine our needs.

Martha often gets a bad rap—as if she were the uptight, spiritually clueless one. But her approach to Jesus didn't indicate that she was spiritually obtuse or insensitive. I believe Martha had sized up the situation according to the way God wired her, and she was moving in her ministry gift of hospitality. When Christ said, "Martha, you are worried about so many things," He wasn't slamming her agenda, just readjusting her priorities. When Jesus goes on to say that Mary had chosen the best thing, it was not to undercut Martha's role as hostess but to help her understand the very crux of life: communion with Himself.

Jesus was actually summoning Martha to a place of release. It was as if He were saying, "Martha, I know what you really need. Let Me take the burden from you." Martha was not aware of her needs, so she could not define them. But the worry she expressed sprang both from a proper sense of diligence and from a need she could not define. Therefore, Jesus came to her and said, "Your heart is longing for something else that is not to be found in fussing with food and dishes. Let me release you and help you define your longings and then show you that I am the One who meets those longings." This was not a rebuke but a summons to joy. Jesus was helping Martha discover her "escape hatch."

This account shows that prayer is never meant to produce feelings of guilt; it is meant to always produce a sense of rest and evoke images of joy. We seem prone to beating ourselves over the head when it comes to this exercise of prayer, but perhaps our focus needs to be more on getting thirsty for God than on condemning ourselves.

The psalmist sketches a poignant picture of the thirsting soul: "As the deer pants for streams of water, so my soul pants for you, O God. My soul thirsts for God, for the living God" (Psalm 42:1–2). The picture of the thirsting soul seeking God fits neatly in our image of what is spiritual. This is the domain of those who have traveled much farther on perfection's road than we. The earnest seeker whose inner sensitivities are pitched to a much higher degree than ours seems more like a religious icon than anyone to whom we, the earthbound weighted down with everyday concerns, could relate.

Perhaps we have romanticized this picture of the thirsting soul and in so doing have conveniently distanced ourselves from true spirituality—leaving intimacy with God to only the few who we believe have been "called." To many, this picture of earnestness only reminds them of the discouragements unsurmounted, the anxieties unanswered, the depression unchecked, and the fears unconquered.

After all, only the holy are thirsty for God.

But I think we have misread what the psalmist was expressing. For here he is, drawing a comparison between a deer pant-

ing for water and a soul longing for God. Is a panting deer a picture of mature development or of superior animal intelligence?
Of course not! It is simply the evidence of a basic survival
instinct. Nothing amazing about that. The animal's body has a
built-in mechanism: In the absence of proper fluid it's going to
thirst. It's a part of the animal's nature.

The same holds true for us when despair or anxiety pinches
our emotions. When we don't have enough of God, we sense
despair, hopelessness, or fear. There's nothing superspiritual
about this. It's just basic survival instinct. We shouldn't look at
depression as a sin nor even just a sickness but as a thirst for
God. We shouldn't look at inner stress as a mark of spiritual
immaturity but as a thirst for God.

These emotional states can be *occasion* for sin, for the enemy
is only too ready to exploit these weaknesses and sow unbelief
into our souls. The sin comes when we let these anxieties
become altars, which allows unbelief to dominate. If we fail to
see these things as spiritual thirst, our spiritual appetites are
quickly deadened. We must make certain we don't let the
enemy accuse us of lapses in our spiritual fervor, but rather see
these things as indications of spiritual dehydration.

"Blessed are those who hunger and thirst for righteousness,"
Jesus said, "for they will be filled" (Matthew 5:6). We can easily
regard this passage as a state of spirituality too lofty for us to
attain. But here again we need to see the hunger not as having
arrived at a level of inner discipline unknown to those of us who
punch computers, fight traffic, and change diapers, but as the natural appetite that emerges when we've neglected righteousness.
We need to see it as hunger in the face of guilt. For guilt is not to

be avoided or rationalized away. Neither should we allow it to threaten us. Guilt too can be an expression of spiritual hunger if we let it.

When we feel guilty for not having prayed, we should see that guilt as something we can use more constructively—an indication of hunger and thirst for God rather than a reminder of our spiritual ineptness. We should come humbly before the Lord, grateful for the grace in which we stand, and allow the guilt to push us *toward* Him.

Calvin Miller tells the story of the early spiritual journey of St. Theresa:

> When she first joined the Carmelites, she prayed that God would make her pray for hours every day, as though much rigorous prayer was the quintessence of devotion. God gave her no such schedule. What He did was give her an appetite for Himself, and once hunger for God was whetted, she prayed without ceasing.[5]

When we let God whet our appetite, prayer will not just be a discipline. It will be a pleasure.

intimacy with god—
Having Ears to Hear

I was winging my way on a red-eye from London to Chicago. Exhausted and hoping to find a row of empty seats where I could stretch out and snooze, I quickly combed the cabin. This was some years ago, when you could still *find* empty seats on an airplane, and I was able to snatch an entire middle section on that 747. Once the plane was airborne, I made myself a comfy pallet and was soon in la-la land. I awakened several hours later, groggy and disoriented. As I motioned to the flight attendant for a cup of coffee, I noticed three men sitting behind me about four rows back.

I had just closed my eyes wishing I could grab another hour of sleep when these words came forcefully into my mind: *The men behind you belong to a rock band, and I want you to go and tell them about Me.* What was this? I thought that I might be in that twilight zone between sleep and wakefulness, so I pushed the words out of my mind.

"I need some coffee," I said to myself.

The words came to me again even more forcefully, and again

I ignored them. *I can't go back there and ask three total strangers if they're in a rock band,* I thought. The flight attendant finally served me some coffee. I was between gulps when that little voice spoke once more into my mind: *Those men are members of a rock band, and I want you to go tell them about Me.* This time I could not blame my grogginess. The words were accompanied by a sense of curiosity and even excitement.

"I guess there's no harm in engaging them in some friendly conversation," I said to myself. So I summoned whatever moxie I had, and sauntered over to talk to them.

"Excuse me," I said haltingly, "but are you guys part of a rock and roll band?"

"Oh yeah," the one nearest to me replied. "We're members of the Ozzy Osbourne band."

BINGO! All my senses were tuned to a high pitch now.

My courage skyrocketed because I knew that I had heard the word of the Lord. And if God so clearly gave me information in a supernatural way, surely He would enable me to share the gospel with these men. For the next forty-five minutes I was like John the Baptist, "a man sent from God," for those rockers. I held nothing back. I laid out the gospel in very clear terms, and they responded with the usual "If God is a God of love, why is there war and suffering" sort of stuff, to which I was able to give clear and concise answers. Hearing the Spirit's voice and partnering with Him in this adventure thrilled me to my core.

It was an exciting and exhilarating episode in my spiritual life, and it happened because I was able to discern the voice of my heavenly Father.

KNOWING HIS VOICE

This business about hearing God's voice is not complicated. It really boils down to learning how to differentiate between Satan's voice, our own voice, and God's voice. That is where so much confusion lies. How do we know if impressions that come into our minds are from the Lord or if they are random thoughts?

There are three steps we should take to cultivate sensitivity to His voice. First, we need to build the apparatus that allows us to hear God's voice. Second, we need to know how to use that apparatus to hear His voice in *specific* situations. And third, we need to be able to test whether or not what we are hearing is actually from God.

Before we examine these steps, let me put your mind at ease about a few things. First, God speaks to His children in a variety of ways—through circumstances, through others, through nature, through dreams (though this method must be tethered to sound biblical instruction). And He *always* speaks to us through the Scriptures.

Second, the way God speaks to certain people often corresponds to the way He has wired them. Someone who is more reflective and contemplative by nature may find it easier to hear the "still small voice" than someone who is more the "action-Jackson" type. King David could certainly hear the whispering of heaven—but he was also content to receive the word of the Lord through another, without questioning his own intimacy with God.

Third, we must avoid valuing certain methods of guidance over others—for example, visions over godly counsel—lest we introduce a contagion of legalism whereby we measure spirituality by the degree to which someone's mode of guidance rings with what we consider supernatural overtones. Those who may not *hear* from God as directly as others must never be made to feel spiritually unqualified.

Dallas Willard warns us that we mustn't frame divine guidance in such a way as to "place sincere Christians on the outside looking in. It is not necessarily that their experience is lacking, but [that] they do not know the language or how the experience works. This leaves them confused and deficient…it undermines their confidence that they are fully acceptable to God."[1]

Fourth, we need to understand that God desires firsthand relationships with us. Many people, fearful of actually hearing His voice, feel that God will guide them only in an indirect way; so they trust Him to lead them only by circumstances. This fear is often rooted in their uncertainty about the origin of the impressions. But God doesn't want to lead us only through circumstances. He, like any father who loves his children, wants to communicate directly. As Fredrick William Faber says, "There is hardly ever a complete silence in our soul. God is whispering to us well-nigh incessantly."[2]

Again, Dallas Willard takes a friendly jab at those of us who retreat from the idea that God wants to communicate with His children directly: "The Spirit is not mute, restricting himself to an occasional nudge, a hot flash, a brilliant image or a case of goosebumps."[3]

Consider the following illustration: Let's say a dad wants his teenage son to do some work on the car. To convey his wishes, he places bits and pieces of the car's motor in places where his son will obviously see them. Upon arising, the youth stumbles out of his bedroom and trips over a crankshaft, goes into the bathroom and sees a piston, then bops into the kitchen to find a carburetor lying on the table. Then, before going out the door, he sees an alternator belt. By that time, he may get the idea that his dad wants him to do something about the car.

That would be a ridiculous way for a father to communicate to his son. If he wants the car fixed, he would *speak* to his son and directly tell him what he wanted. This, of course, would underscore the health of that relationship. The father and son should know how to communicate. Our heavenly Father loves us infinitely more than even the most loving earthly fathers and longs to commune with us heart to heart.

FRAMING A HOUSE, DRAWING A LANDSCAPE

Recently, actor Richard Dreyfuss, appearing on the BRAVO channel, observed, "Life is a journey from certainty to confusion." For many, attempts at "hearing God" feel that way. At first, they feel confident that God loves them and speaks to them. But then they lose their bearings somewhat and start wondering whose voice they're hearing.

Hearing God is not a precise science, and we will ever be cultivating a more keen sensitivity to His voice. It is a lifelong learning adventure. Yet there are things we can do to construct a foundation upon which we can build a structure of principles that will provide "a home" in which we can have communion with God.

Diligence in the Word

Of course, God can and will speak to the most recently converted. Hearing God is not the domain of the mature. If it were, sensitivity to God would be perceived as the product of our pursuit of spiritual perfection. For example, we may ill advisedly connect an ability to hear God to the length of our prayers. In other words, if we pray more we will hear better. Thus, prayer would cease to be a joyous response to God and would instead become a means of procuring spiritual sensitivity. Our focus would then shift from God to our spiritual maturity.

Having said that, I would like to stress that as we grow we should quite naturally develop a greater appetite for the Word. Hunger for God and hunger for His Word go hand in hand. The Word becomes an essential part of the foundation we build upon so we can properly establish the structure that houses our communion with God. This part of our structure is important, for the more Scripture we get into our minds, the more effective our mental filter will be when it comes to sifting impressions.

For example, let's say a believer is confronted with a public school supervisor attempting to surreptitiously introduce outrageous, anti-Christian material into a school's curricula. Alarmed at that news, the believer prays for some insight from the Lord as to how to respond, but cannot get beyond his initial feelings of anger. Is the anger from God? From Satan? Is it just a natural response of the offense that person feels? Or is it perhaps a mixture of the three?

At first, we may want to reject such an angry response as being not in keeping with the biblical precept "Forgive your enemies." But one more richly steeped in the Word will also take into account passages from the Psalms that talk about a righ-teous, vigorous anger directed not toward people but toward unrighteousness. The anger the believer feels toward the school supervisor may very well have God in it, but one who knows the Word will know how to sift that impression like a miner panning for gold. One who knows the Scriptures will be better able to locate the pure gold of the Lord's Word, while discard-ing the sand of human response.

Many are suspicious of the idea that people can hear God personally. They have seen imbalances, excesses, even down-right deception. They have seen people doing things "in the name of the Lord" that appear provocative or inappropriate (although, in more than a few instances, God has asked me to do things that seem to run against the grain of social conven-tion). But these fears needn't keep us from fully enjoying the still, small voice of God. The knowledge of the Bible acts as a safeguard against deception, a sieve through which we sift mental impressions.

Rightly relating to authority

Centuries ago, four monks traveled from Scete to visit a revered spiritual father by the name of Abba Pambo. He asked each of them to describe the goodness of the others, though not in one another's presence. They separately explained that one of them fasted much, one of them had given up all material goods, and the third was a man of great charity. Of the fourth, they said that he had lived in obedience to the elders for twenty-two years.

Abba Pambo told them: "I tell you, this last is a greater virtue than the others. Each of you others has to use his own will to keep his virtue. But [this fourth] monk irradicates [sic] his self will and makes himself the servant of another's will. Men like that, if they persevere until death are confessors," meaning that those who truly understand proper submission to authority will in the end become the most trusted.[4]

It is impossible to address the subject of rightly relating to authority in just a few short paragraphs. Nevertheless, it must be mentioned here.

Each of us needs to be under some authority. We all need people who will tell us no. If our appetites are never curbed, our wills never crossed, we will never be able to trust that the impressions we receive are actually from God. If we are not accustomed to accountability, if we haven't become comfortable with being told no, then we will not develop the ability to discern when our flesh is sanctioning our desires. It is easy to rationalize and convince ourselves that what we want is what God wants—when in reality we are doing what we want and slapping God's name on it.

For example, it can be difficult to check our desires at the door when we ask the Lord for guidance in buying that new car, attending that college, or pursuing that romantic relationship. Yet, when we graciously accept the boundaries set by those in authority over us, we are able to exercise authority over our own emotions and say no when we are faced with a critical decision.

Whether it's a parent, a pastor, or a president, we need those in our lives who have the authority to say no. There will never be a time in our lives when we don't need to be under authority in some way.

We also need to express and receive what I call *alongside*

authority. We don't need just to walk *under* certain authorities, but also walk *with* certain people in whose lives we can make a difference. There should always be people in our lives—friends, working associates, fellow students—with whom we can reciprocate influence. These lateral accountability relationships are extremely helpful because buddies can often correct us in a less threatening manner than those that are above us.

Rightly relating to the authority of the Word and the authority of people creates for us the inner structure that helps us implement the principles that help us hear God. Yet there is one more critical chunk of material we need.

An understanding of grace

One of the most consoling passages on guidance in the New Testament is John 10, in which Jesus says, "My sheep know my voice" (vv. 14–16). Jesus wasn't stressing the sheep's struggle to follow, but the certainty of the Shepherd's ability to lead. He wasn't stressing the ability of the sheep to hear the Shepherd's voice, but the Shepherd's ability to make His voice clear.

Would a sheep following a shepherd anxiously wonder whether it was hearing the shepherd's voice, the wolf's voice, or its own *baas*? Obviously not! Sheep simply follow their shepherd, just as we as God's sheep are to follow our Shepherd. This is simple because the grace of God is at work. When we don't have a grasp on God's grace, our attempts to hear His voice ensnare us in anxiety. Believing that we can't hear Him, we conclude that we must not be spiritual enough.

Grace keeps us from the kind of legalism that causes us to somehow measure His favor by our own spiritual performance.

In light of this, it is actually comforting that Jesus compares us to one of the dumbest of animals. If sheep can hear, so can we!

Grace not only allows us to hear God's voice, but it also gives us hearts to follow His leading.

A friend of mine when he was young once told the Lord, "Lord, I'll minister anywhere but Africa. Please don't send me to Africa." The Lord did not beat him over the head with a stick. Instead, He worked with him and slowly changed his heart. A few years later, my friend found himself kneeling by his bedside and crying for God to move mightily in Africa. He actually expressed to God a desire to go there himself. Suddenly he bolted upright. He realized that God had changed his heart! He remembered his earlier prayers that God not send him to Africa. Now he was begging God to let him go.

That's what happens to a heart that is touched by the grace of God. Grace gives us the ability to hear our Master's voice, and it changes our *have-to*s to *want-to*s.

Again and again our Lord Jesus enjoins the churches in Revelation to have ears to hear. Amid the cacophony of distractions in our world, we can nurture a keen sensitivity to His voice. When I discovered that I could actually *hear* Him, my heart began to party—and it has been partying ever since.

CHAPTER 9

Intimacy with god— Listening to His Voice

The tragedy is that our eternal welfare depends upon our hearing,
and we have trained our ears not to hear.

A. W. TOZER

Hours before our youngest was born, I was roaming the concourse at Philadelphia's international airport. My wife, Nancy, was *exceedingly* ready to deliver, but so far hadn't even hinted at labor pains. The doctor told us on a Friday that he would induce the following Monday and that I could proceed with plans to speak at a conference in Harrisburg that weekend.

I was hesitant—we had just moved to Nashville from San Jose, California, and we hardly knew anyone in town. *What if she goes into labor, and I'm not here?* I wondered. *Who can she turn to?*

But the doctor assured me all was well and that the chances of Nancy going into labor before Monday were remote. So I boarded the plane and got as far as Philadelphia. Before catching my connection, I began to feel very uneasy. I thought the Lord was telling me that our baby's birth was imminent, and that I was to take the next flight home. I called my wife and asked her if she was close. "No," she said, "there's no indication that the baby is coming any time soon." She urged me to fly on to the conference. I was a plenary speaker, and to cancel hours before a major conference—well, it just isn't done.

But I couldn't shake the feeling. Finally, I found a quiet corner in baggage claim—as quiet as there is in such a setting—and listened to the Spirit's voice. Within minutes, I was convinced I had to return home. I called the conference host, explained my situation, and flew home. Within a few hours of deplaning, Nancy's water suddenly broke. The baby came—Saturday night! I coached her through her labor, and together we celebrated our third little gift from God. Had I ignored those impressions at the airport, Nancy would have been alone at the delivery of our child.

Hearing God Speak

As I said in the last chapter, the real secret to hearing God is eliminating all other voices and impressions except His. Hearing God's voice can be seen from two angles: receiving divine guidance when we intentionally bring a decision before the Lord and ask Him for specific answers, and knowing how to test impressions that come into our mind on a daily basis. These different disciplines to hearing God require us to apply different principles for each.

Divine guidance

When we come to the Lord specifically to hear Him speak, we can implement the following basic principles, which I received from Joy Dawson, one of my mentors, and which have greatly aided me during my walk with God.

We must yield ourselves to the Holy Spirit. As we have seen, the process of yielding includes the worship and adoration of God, which prepare our hearts to hear from Him. As we worship Him, we need to fulfill this injunction from James: "Submit yourselves, then, to God" (James 4:7). We need to say to the Holy Spirit, "I yield myself to You in this moment of decision. I want only that which will glorify Jesus." By doing this, we align ourselves with the great aim of the Holy Spirit, and that is to exalt Jesus. The Holy Spirit will most definitely answer that request.

As we yield to the Holy Spirit, we need to ask Him to show us sin in our lives that is keeping us from hearing God's voice. There are several Scriptures that suggest that harboring sin erects barriers between us and God. Psalm 66:18 says, "If I regard iniquity in my heart, the Lord will not hear me" (kjv). Isaiah 59:2 states, "But your iniquities have separated you from your God; your sins have hidden his face from you, so that he will not hear."

It's true that sin keeps us from hearing God and God from hearing us, but let's understand it in context. To be justified by God means, in part, that He has accepted us unconditionally, knowing full well all the sins we are going to commit. Our sin does not catch God by surprise, and His expression of revulsion in these two verses is His way of underscoring for us the destructiveness of sin, not His petty offense towards us.

Lamentations 3:44 says, "You have covered yourself with a cloud so that no prayer can get through." This is actually an act of love on God's part, because those feelings that our prayers aren't "getting through" may be the Holy Spirit telling us that something is awry in our lives.

It is important to make some distinctions here. In our desperation to hear God speak, we can jump ahead and begin looking for any sins or attitudes that keep us from hearing from Him. We must remember that though Scripture states that unconfessed sin results in our inability to hear Him, we still remain righteous before the Lord. Because we have been declared righteous, we no longer must deal with sin to gain access to God's presence. Rather, we are now free to deal with sin *in* God's presence.

That perspective is all-important, for it goes to the issue of our security in God. I like what one of my coworkers said to me on this point. She said that when she seeks God on an issue, she doesn't go looking for her sin. Rather, she just spends time worshiping the Lord and focusing on Him, thus allowing the Holy Spirit to identify any sin.

The Holy Spirit wants to reveal junk in our hearts more than we want to have it revealed. Therefore, we don't need to go looking for sin; we just need to keep looking at Jesus and worshiping Him. When He brings sin to our attention, we can confess it and move on, knowing that the blood of Jesus cleanses us from all unrighteousness. If the issue He brings to our minds requires some restitution—making it right with someone—we simply follow through on it as soon as we can.

It should be noted that the psalmist said that "if I *regard* iniquity in my heart, the Lord will not hear" (66:18, emphasis added). This word does not apply to sin in general, but to those sins we know are there but stubbornly refuse to confront. The psalmist wasn't talking about attitudes we don't see or actions we've forgotten.

As we wait on the Holy Spirit, we must give Him adequate time to identify in us those things that grieve Him and keep us from hearing Him. If we are not accustomed to doing this, we may need to spend a half hour with a pad and paper, just waiting on God to bring things to the surface. However, if we are used to coming before the Lord for a daily cleansing, then we may not need to spend as much time waiting on God to reveal sin.

We must also learn to distinguish between conviction and condemnation. When the Lord convicts, He gives us a sense of hope and the motivation to change. The conviction may sting a little, but it will be accompanied by the joys of deeper companionship with Jesus. Such hope inspirits us to follow through with confession and repentance. Condemnation, on the other hand, conveys a sense of defeat and hopelessness—a sense of God's intense displeasure with *us,* rather than with the sin itself. This is a tactic the devil employs often, and we need to be aware of it.

We need to silence the devil's voice. Here we come to the process of eliminating all other voices except God's, and the first voice we must eliminate is Satan's. We know that he wages war in our minds. We know that he can counterfeit the Spirit's voice and give us a false peace. We know he can throw us off balance by interjecting fear into a situation we're praying about. Yet when we come before the Lord for specific guidance, we can follow the latter part of James 4:7, which says, "Resist the devil, and he will flee from you."

We must remember that we have the power to resist the devil only when we have first yielded to the Holy Spirit. We must also remember to resist the devil using the Word of God, even as Jesus did when He was tempted in the wilderness (Matthew 4:4, 7, 10). There are many Scriptures we can stand on as we remind the enemy of our authority in Christ: 2 Corinthians 10:3–4; Isaiah 54:17; and Luke 10:19 are but a few of them.

There is never a need to rant and rave at the enemy, and we must remember the injunction in Jude that we are not to deal frivolously with demonic powers (1:8–9). Nevertheless, we can and ought to deal with the enemy directly by the word of Scripture and in the name of Jesus—according to our righteous standing in Him by virtue of His shed blood. We can do this with the full conviction that "greater is He who is in you than he who is in the world" (1 John 4:4, NASB).

It is by resisting the enemy, according to the Scriptures, that the devil and his minions will leave us. This was true in Christ's example. After successfully resisting Satan, Satan "departed from Him for a season" (Luke 4:13, KJV). This doesn't mean Jesus no longer endured temptation, only that the voice of darkness was silenced for a time. In the same way, we can be assured that during those moments when we wait on the Lord, the enemy cannot counterfeit the voice of God, cannot distort the Word of God, and cannot introduce any wrong impression into our minds.

We must silence our own voice. This step may be the most critical of them all, for most of the time, this is where the real battle lies. In fact, the enemy often doesn't have to attack our minds because he can sit back and allow our own fleshly desires to bend our thoughts toward our own will. Here is where many believers become discouraged. "Can I really silence my own voice?" they ask. I believe that we can, at least momentarily, when we wait on God.

In seeking Him, it is important to focus on ourselves and bring our will into conformity with His will. We do that by first acknowledging that our thoughts and ways are not His (see

Isaiah 55:8), then by expressing our desire that God, in a particular moment of guidance, impose His thoughts on ours. In short, we express our deepest desire to die to our own imaginations, thoughts, reasons, desires, feelings. This requires great faith, especially if our feelings and emotions are stacking the deck toward one answer over another. Reining our feelings in is no easy business. But we can trust the Lord to silence our own voice in that moment of time.

HEARING GOD SPEAK!

As I said earlier, the Lord speaks in many ways—through dreams, through visions, through circumstances, through our leaders, and through nature. Ken Gire calls these and many other modes of divine communication "windows of the soul."

> We must always be looking and listening if we are to
> see the windows and hear what is being spoken to us
> through them…windows are everywhere, and at any
> time we may find one.[1]

God can speak in a variety of ways, but I want to focus here on the Spirit's still, small voice and on the word of Scripture because these are the basic means of hearing Him, and they reflect a more intimate side of guidance.

Having eliminated the enemy's voice and our own voice, we are now ready to hear God's voice. However, before we go off half-cocked thinking that because we've silenced the devil and ourselves, any impression we receive must be from God, we must humble ourselves and test the impressions or voices we hear. And the best way to test these things is to be familiar with the "still small voice" and with Scripture.

The still small voice

One of the classic texts on God's "still small voice" is Colossians 3:15: "Let the peace of Christ rule in your hearts."

This verse gives the sense that the Holy Spirit acts as an arbiter that resolves conflicting impressions or opinions, or as an umpire that indicates whether we are safe or out when we seek His will about a given decision. He aids us by giving us a simple yes or no, or by giving us a sense of peace or dis-peace.

If, for example, we are seeking God about a certain item to purchase, we may, having gone through the steps of eliminating "other" voices, receive a simple unsettling in our heart. This can mean one of two things: Either the Holy Spirit is checking us— telling us that it would be unwise to purchase this particular article—or He is saying wait, that it is not His time to reveal an answer either way.

Of course, it is wise to avoid what Dallas Willard calls the "message-a-minute" view of divine guidance, meaning praying about everything from what we wear in the morning to what kind of gas we put in our car.[2] Such hyperspirituality trivializes the gift of hearing His voice and defies the God-graced natural-ness of life.

The Word

At times, the Lord actually uses Scriptures to give us specific insights. When I was a teenager, God dramatically reinforced the fact that He can use Scripture to give specific guidance. I was sixteen, and I had begun to seek the Lord earnestly. One warm July night, I felt the Lord prompt me to go on a three-day fast. Almost immediately I felt a strong impression to turn to Haggai 2. Like most sixteen-year-olds, I had no idea what was in Haggai. I was tired so I went to bed without looking up the Scripture.

The next day I began my fast. Later that morning I again felt a strong urge to read Haggai 2. I quickly turned to that passage and read these words: "On the twenty-first day of the seventh month, the word of the LORD came…. '[Begin the] work'" (vv. 1, 4). Adrenaline shot through my body, and I ran to the kitchen calendar and checked the date. The day before had been July 21, the twenty-first day of the seventh month. And it was at eleven-thirty that night in which the Lord had told me to turn to Haggai 2. Such a dramatic confirmation that I was to begin my fast rocketed me into the spiritual stratosphere. It was during those three days of fasting that I received my call to spiritual leadership.

Not all guidance confirmed by a Scripture verse is this dramatic. We must be cautious and judicious when we ask God for confirming Scriptures. Though the Word can be a rich source of guidance, we must remember the following caveats:

Don't read too much into Scripture. It will be obvious when God gives you a Scripture that has a bearing on the matter at hand. There will be no need to wrestle from the text a meaning that is not there.

Don't assume God isn't speaking. If we receive a Scripture that bears no connection to the issue we are praying about, it doesn't mean God hasn't spoken. On the contrary, it may be an indication that it is not His time to reveal an answer. We should diligently seek God, but never push to get answers. Oswald Chambers wisely counsels, "Never run before God's guidance. If there is the slightest doubt, then He is not guiding. Whenever there is doubt—*don't.*"[3]

Never play Bible roulette. Never just open your Bible, see where your eyes land, and pick a verse at random. That bears more resemblance to sorcery than it does seeking God.

Never go on the Scripture verse or passage alone. If God gives you a specific Scripture, it is only one of several confirmations you need for guidance. More on this later.

T E S T I N G   W H A T   W E   H E A R

Because listening to God is so personal, because hearing Him accurately is such an important measurement of our intimacy with Him, we are often reluctant to test what we hear. We fear that if we place our impressions under scrutiny, we'll find our spiritual sensitivity wanting. *If I'm not hearing accurately,* we reason, *I must not be as close to God as I thought.* Consequently, to test our words is to court the possibility of disillusionment. But deception is vastly worse than disillusionment, so it behooves us to vigorously examine our guidance. Besides, testing what we hear enhances our discernment of the Master's voice.

There are two contexts of divine guidance in which we should develop biblical filters. The first is in the actual pursuit of divine guidance. The second is how we test spontaneous impressions we receive. As we test our guidance, we need to tether ourselves to four key confirmations:

- the green light of peace (Colossians 3:16);
- the green light of confirming Scripture;
- the green light of confirming circumstances;
- the green light that comes from accountable relationships, especially those under whose leadership God has placed us.

Remember: The greater the issue—marriage, career, college choice—the more we need to reference all these green lights.

The second of these contexts—receiving impressions from His still small voice—requires a different kind of filtering system. Obviously, if we think we hear God telling us to talk to a stranger on the bus, we don't have time to go to an authority figure or to wait for a confirming Scripture. We have to act quickly before the bus stops.

God wants to talk to us. But He also wants us to carefully test our impressions. So how do we evaluate impressions that come to our minds?

First, if the impression is from the Holy Spirit, we will receive a growing sense of joy and confidence in the repeated urgings that come to our minds. If after a few moments of pondering we sense more fear than faith, chances are it isn't God speaking. Hannah Whitall Smith, in her book *The Christian's Secret of a Happy Life,* puts it this way: "If the suggestion is from Him, it will continue and strengthen; if it is not from Him, it will disappear and we shall almost forget we ever had it."[4]

Second, as we wait on God for quick confirmation, we can send up "bullet prayers," like Nehemiah did (Nehemiah 2:4), asking Him to bring to mind a confirming passage of Scripture that tells us which course to take. This is one reason it is so important to commit Scripture to memory. The more Scripture we know, the deeper the well the Spirit can draw from to give us on-the-spot guidance.

Hearing God's Voice: It's for All of Us!

Many Christians think that sensitivity to God's voice is the domain of only the most saintly. But hearing Him is the privilege of every one of His children.

Frank Buchman was one of the spiritual giants of the twentieth century. He was founder of the Moral Rearmament Movement, counselor to presidents and kings—he even played a significant role in the rebuilding of Europe after World War II.

Buchman was intense about Christ—and about listening to His voice, which he called "that arresting tick" that could intrude into a person's ordinary thinking with particular authority. Buchman succinctly summarizes the simplicity of hearing God's voice:

Listening means an unhurried time when God really can have a chance to imprint His thoughts in your mind. Some days it is simply a series of luminous thoughts of things God wants me to do that day. Some days it is just a sense of peace and rest and one or two outstanding things. Other days, it is a sense of need for intercession on behalf of certain people. It takes all the fret, strain, and worry out of life. *This listening to God is not the experience of a few men…it is the most sane, normal, healthful thing a person can do.*[5]

Sane, normal, healthy. God never intended us to respond to His guidance like mice in a maze, eventually getting to where He wants us but encountering bumps and detours along the way. He is a Father who wants to commune with His children, a Shepherd who is able to lead each one of His sheep, a Lover who wants to make His voice known more than we could ever want to know it.

CHAPTER 10

The freedom of a Life of praise

Praise creates a dwelling place for God in man's present situation.
JACK HAYFORD

A pastor friend of mine in Sydney recently recounted a most interesting story that illustrates the power of praise. He and a missionary were on a trek through the outback of Australia and got their truck stuck deep in cow manure. The missionary got underneath the truck and tried to create some traction for the tires by wedging a board between them and the mud. With each attempt, the man sank deeper into the fetid sludge. After several efforts he was exhausted, covered with cow dung, and overcome by the stench and the flies. All this and not a soul within miles.

So he began to praise the Lord—full throttle, at the top of his lungs.

It must have been a comical scene: a seasoned missionary, a dignified pastor, a truck sunk in manure up to its axle—and the sounds of praise!

Unknown to them, a group of Aborigines had spontaneously decided to go on a walk that, as it turned out, led them close to the scene of the mishap. This was wilderness area, and none of the natives expected to find any hint of outsiders. They would have passed the pastor and missionary by, except for the singing that caught their ears. When they heard the two men singing and praising God, they ran toward the sound and came upon the men and the stuck truck. After a friendly greeting, the Aborigines quickly helped them out of their muddy mess.

As he finished his story, this pastor, now gray with years, leaned across the table to me and with a spark of merriment in his eyes said, "It just goes to show that when we are neck deep in manure, praise is the way out!"

Psalm 100 tells us to "enter his gates with thanksgiving and his courts with praise." This psalm is the climax of a series of jubilee psalms that start with Psalm 93. Read together, these songs are intended to free the worshiper to celebrate the power and goodness of God, even in the face of adverse circumstances. Psalm 95 tells us to sing joyfully unto the Lord because He holds all things in the palm of His hand (v. 4). Most of us enjoy singing that old spiritual "He's Got the Whole World in His Hands," but I wonder if we really believe it.

The great enemy of praise and the primary root of complaining—and its kissing cousins: frustration, rudeness, and impatience—is unbelief.

God hated the murmuring of Israel because He knew it would engender a culture of complaint. And God still hates murmuring and complaining. It seems so harmless to fuss about this or that, to spew mild little grumblings about the neighbor's dog, the stock market's dip, or the boss's surly attitude. In fact, little complaints mumbled under our breath seem almost therapeutic in a way. At least we've gotten it off our chest and externalized our emotions rather than internalizing them. The last thing any of us would want to do is copy the Stoic, gamely absorbing life's blows in silent, if tortured, acquiescence.

But complaining inevitably leads to impatience. In fact, impatience seems to feed off of the tiny little complaints we emit. Complaining reinforces the negatives that frustrate us, causing us to become rude, irritable, and overly self-focused. When we grumble and complain, we are ultimately imprisoned by feelings of confinement, powerlessness, and discouragement.

God invites us to praise Him rather than complain, because to do so frees us. For to praise Him is to affirm His control over the world. After all, if He is in control, why worry?

Praise is the recognition of His sovereignty, which infuses our lives with joy unspeakable.

THE BLESSINGS OF PRAISE

God calls us to praise Him because He wants to bless us. Consider the benefits that multiply to us when we praise the Lord.

Praise opens us to wisdom. When the psalmist summons us to praise God because He is in control of all things, he is drawing a relationship between our praise and our recognition of God's sovereignty.

If we truly believe that God holds the whole world in His hands, then we will respond with a never-ending gush of praise and thanksgiving. The converse of this is true as well. If I find myself not praising the Lord—even grumbling and ungrateful—it is likely because I have lost my confidence in Him. These attitudes show that I have been so seduced by a cultural mindset that puts a high premium on free choice, that over time I have come to believe that the power of my freedom and others' freedom is greater than that of God.

We all want to believe in God's overriding control, but all too often we feel like victims of others' bad choices. *If only my employer hadn't done this* or *if only my spouse hadn't done that,* we think. This attitude can ring true when it comes to the bad choices *we've* made. We feel that we are disqualified from enjoying God's blessings because of repeated sins and bad judgment.

"Just praise Me," the Lord says, "and see if I don't reveal to you My sovereignty. Praise Me and see if I don't make sense out of life for you." Indeed, God works all things together for good (see Romans 8:28). God's invitation to praise Him in all things, to rejoice and again rejoice (Philippians 4:4), is an open invitation to wisdom. On the other hand, complaining cuts us off from His wisdom, and thus life seems random; the actions and choices of others seem to thwart our game plan and jeopardize our joy.

Praise opens us to faith. To praise God is to recognize that He is in absolute control. That's what it means to have faith—realizing that the choices others make, or even our own wrong choices, cannot keep us from our destiny as long as we "come into the light," repent, and go on. In fact, it's not necessarily our bad choices that keep us from our destiny, but rather blindness to God's redeeming power. Remember, to say that God is our redeemer is to say that what has been lost—the missed opportunity, the lost time, the broken relationship—can be recovered, redeemed in such a way that our ultimate destiny in Him is not jeopardized.

This is one reason why praising God is so important. It opens us to see redemptive possibilities. Praise keeps us constantly tuned to the reality of God's sovereignty, which in turn opens us to faith. And remember, whatever is not of faith cannot please God. Hence, one of the great keys to faith is praise. So notice the progression:

> Praise opens us up to the reality of God's *sovereignty*,
> which gives us a glimpse of His *wisdom*,
> which in turn breeds *faith* within us,
> > which imbues us with the *confidence*
> > > to make right choices,
> > which then propels us on to our
> > > *destiny and purpose in God.*

The more we praise, the more we see; and the more we see, the more we understand how God is working everything for our good. The more we see Him working things together for our good, the greater our faith; and the greater our faith, the more we praise. Praise and faith feed off each other, just as complaining and unbelief do.

Fanning the flames of praise fans the flame of faith. The Israelites needed to know how to trust God beyond the reality of their circumstances. They needed to know how to stand firm against imposing cities with unscalable walls, giants twice their size, and entrenched demonic cultures.

A lifestyle of praise was meant to keep the Israelites open to the wisdom of God so when they came to challenges like Jericho, they could respond to God's ways, not man's. Jericho, if you recall, was the first city Joshua and the Israelites confronted in their conquest of the Promised Land. With its high, thick walls it seemed impenetrable. But instead of instructing them to utilize conventional military tactics, God commanded them to march around the walls—for seven days! When they completed their assignment, the city fell before them.

We often look at the story of Jericho in terms of Joshua's courage to do the unconventional and the seemingly absurd. But let's look at it a different way. For years, the Israelites had been doing one thing: walking. When it came to Jericho, it's as if God said, "Just keep walking. Don't try to do anything in your own strength or by your own initiatives. Don't try to take this city doing anything different from what I have had you doing. I've had you walk across the desert; now walk around this city."

In a sense, this was God's way of calling them to that place of rest, that place where God Himself takes the city. Of course, after Jericho the Israelites engaged in armed conflict. But their run to the battle was the joyous overflow of confidence in God, confidence fueled by praise.

Praise opens us to freedom. It is precisely at our weakest points that we need to praise the Lord. When things seem black around us, then we must praise! When we feel caught in a mire of depression, then we must praise all the more. Not because praise is a magical incantation that somehow sets us free, but because praise opens our eyes to see what God is doing through our circumstances and what He has been doing all along: showing us that we are not trapped, but free.

Because praise opens us to wisdom, and wisdom cultivates faith, praise thus leads us to freedom. We needn't feel hopeless because of our mistakes, for we know God can redeem what we have lost. For example, it is easy to become discouraged with the ongoing moral decline of our nation. That discouragement can make us critical of the church, negative about our neighborhoods—just all-around grousers. But when we praise Him, we are free to see that the Lord is in control, and we can know that if He allows our nation to continue on its course of deterioration, He, in His love, is simply letting the prodigal eat the husks of pig slop before he returns to the Father.

Of course, praise doesn't absolve us of our responsibility to make a difference in our world, nor should it neutralize our efforts to prophetically impact our culture or confront immorality. Praise illuminates our minds with God's perspective, allowing us to see things *His* way. In fact, real praisers are real activists. They are not disillusioned when they see few results, not put off by a culture's deaf ear to their message, and not easily discouraged by the spiritual apathy and moral complacency around them.

So, note the progression of the benefits of praise:

- Praise opens us up to the reality of God's *sovereignty,*
- which opens us up to *wisdom,*
- which cultivates *faith,*
- which breeds *freedom,*
- which catalyzes genuine *activism.*

So often, we feel neutralized by life. We feel as though we're making little difference; we're trapped, even paralyzed. But praise is the antidote to spiritual paralysis. Paul understood that when he wrote these sonic booms of praise from inside a Roman prison: "Rejoice in the Lord always. I will say it again: Rejoice!...

Do not be anxious about anything…. And the peace of God, which transcends all understanding, will guard your hearts and your minds…. I can do everything through him who gives me strength" (Philippians 4:4, 6–7, 13).

We are to praise God in the midst of hardships because it is praise that jolts us out of our sedation and makes us spiritually alert. Just as caffeine wakens us physically, so praise stimulates our spiritual senses. Praise heightens our sensitivity, opens us up to creativity, and renders us alert to the whispers of God.

So when in doubt, *praise*.

Still, you may ask *how* you are to praise God. Certainly, our words are a vital way to offer praise to God. But there are other ways to praise Him.

POSTURES OF PRAISE

It is helpful to understand how various physical expressions of praise are rooted in Scripture. For example, why do we clap our hands or raise our hands to God? Is there any scriptural valida- tion to this whole idea of "dancing before the Lord"? These questions deserve thoughtful response, for none of us wants to tip the scales of excess or slip into a kind of exuberance where praise is nothing more than an emotional purgative, rather than an expression that glorifies God. On the other hand, few of us would think twice of cheering, full throttle, our favorite football team. Is not God worthy of such enthusiastic response? Of course, as we seek to praise the Lord in the manner worthy of His glory, it is always imperative to root our convictions in bib- lical precedent.

Clapping our hands

When we clap our hands in praise, we are doing far more than just keeping rhythm. The act of clapping the hands before God is rooted in Israelite military custom. It is said that when the Lord directed the ancient Israelites to go to war, He sometimes instructed them to do a very unorthodox thing: clap their hands before Him. Psalm 47, which begins with the celebratory "Clap your hands, all you nations," was most likely written after the miraculous victory God performed over Judah's enemies during Jehoshaphat's reign (see 2 Chronicles 20).[1] Theirs was a victory won literally on the wings of praise, for they overcame without conflict. They "clapped their way" to conquest, simply praising God as He supernaturally routed the enemy.

In the book of Job, we find a different Hebrew word for *clap,* and it is the first time this particular word is used in the Old Testament. In Job 27:23, Job voices his intention to clap his hands in the face of his accusers (NASB).[2] It seems, then, that clapping of hands before God was rooted in part in the idea of militantly resisting an enemy. When we clap our hands in praise, we are actually stating in faith that our victorious Christ has indeed vanquished the enemy, and are presently routing him on our behalf.

Raising our hands

The first time we see the raising of hands in Scripture is in reference to pledge making. We often think that raising our hands is a nice gesture conveying submission and humility. It is that, but it is actually much more.

In Genesis 14, we read the story of Abraham rescuing his nephew Lot. Abraham had allied himself with five kings who together engaged in battle against the four kings who had kidnapped Lot. Having led them to a great victory, Abraham was offered his share of the booty taken from the conquered kings. Scripture says at that point that Abraham lifted up his hand and pledged, "I have raised my hand to the LORD, God Most High, Creator of heaven and earth, and have taken an oath that I will accept nothing belonging to you" (Genesis 14:22–23). Abraham's act of raising his hand evokes a pledge of fidelity.

I submit that the act of raising our hands before the Lord is an expression of our allegiance to Him as well as a reminder to us of our covenant with Him. When my wife and I celebrate our anniversary, we are reminding ourselves of the covenant we made to each other. In the same way, when we lift our hands before the Lord, we are expressing our fidelity and renewing our covenant with Him.

Dancing before the Lord

The idea of dancing before God may be a stretch to some of us, but the Word is rich with images of such celebration. One of the Hebrew words for *rejoice* strongly suggests the idea of dancing in a whirlwind. In fact, in Zephaniah 3:17, "The LORD...rejoices over [us] with singing," the word for *rejoice* means to dance with abandoned exuberance. Indeed, if God dances over us, should we not, at times, dance before Him?

For those of us who come from more reserved traditions, this particular expression may be one that is better offered privately than publicly. Still, we can express ourselves in this way, knowing that we have biblical grounds for it.

Using our bodies as instruments of praise

Let's go back to Romans 12:1 for a minute. This text not only couches the concept of praise and worship in a lifestyle of sacrificial service, but it also intimates that *every* act of worship—including our expressions of praise and adoration—calls for *bodily* response.

This opens the door to a fascinating possibility: *that there is a corresponding act of praise for every revelation of God.* I can recall, when I first learned this, I was kneeling by my bedside reflecting on the fatherhood of God. Suddenly, it was as if I was windswept into a spiritual euphoria. It hit me: The heavenly Father really desires *me! Personally!* Without thinking about it, I found myself wrapping my hands around my body and praising and worshiping God with a sense of abandon. Of course, there's nothing in Scripture that says we are to praise God by wrapping our arms around our body. But it was as if I was trying to capture in physical expression what the Lord was imparting to my heart.

It is scripturally valid to involve one's body in response to God. Again, I quote Richard Foster:

> The Bible describes worship in physical terms. The root meaning of the Hebrew word we translate "worship" is "to prostrate." The word "bless" literally means "to kneel." Thanksgiving refers to "an extension of the

hand." Throughout Scripture we find a variety of physical postures in connection with worship: lying prostrate, standing, kneeling, lifting the hands, clapping the hands, lifting the head, bowing the head, dancing, and wearing sackcloth and ashes. The point is that we are to offer God our bodies as well as all the rest of our being. Worship is appropriately physical.[3]

When we are alone with God and He begins to speak to us and show us more of Himself, there are any number of ways we can express our praise to Him.

A Rule of Thumb: Focus on Jesus!

I need to state an important caveat at this point: When it comes to the corporate expression of our praise and worship—that is, worship within the church setting—there is a principle that seems to guide the apostle Paul's mind when he deals with the issue of proper decorum in believers' gatherings (see 1 Corinthians 14). It is simply this: No individual act of praise should take the focus off of Jesus. In other words, if we are gathered together worshiping and praising God and the rest of the saints are involved in a collective sense of silent reflection, it would be inappropriate for one to suddenly shout his praises aloud. One can imagine that at such an outburst all heads would be turned toward that person, their focus on Christ jarringly interrupted.

The Holy Spirit won't author any expression of praise that takes the congregation's focus off of Jesus. We must always have an ear to the Spirit and an ear to each other so that our corporate worship engenders focus on the Lord. Our gatherings are not occasions for each of us individually to have his own private worship experience. Rather, our gatherings are our opportunity to offer a corporate gift of praise to the Lord. Therefore, we need to keep in step with one another. It is refreshing to see a congregation growing in its sensitivity to the Lord. Such a people will find themselves rising to several expressions of praise and worship that enhance the congregation's focus on Jesus.

Years ago, a rabbi told me that the Israelites knew only two postures of worship: flat on their faces, prostrate before the holiness of the Lord; or standing upright with their hands stretched above their heads as high as they would go, in triumphant celebration of God. These are two very extreme postures of worship, but they speak to the issue of *how they perceived God.* The Israelites must have seen God in such a way that their only appropriate response to Him was the most radical physical response they could express.

How paltry, sometimes, is our praise by comparison!

warring in worship

God's wars are fought to the sound of music and praise!
MICHAEL BROWN

We had gathered simply to praise the Lord. About seven hundred of us. Nothing overpowering—no stacks of fifty-foot-tall amplifiers—just enthusiastic worshipers, a few guitars, and a garage band sound system. It was mid-morning on a Saturday at Union Square, downtown San Francisco. The square is situated in a rather posh shopping district in the city, surrounded by well-known department stores like Macy's and famous hotels like the St. Francis. We had come from all over the Bay Area to spend a week sharing our faith throughout the city.

It all began harmlessly enough. We were there not to provoke anyone or to cause any unrest. We were there simply to worship the Lord publicly. But during the preceding days, word of our presence had leaked to the more radical elements in the city, and you could sense that something was brewing. We began to sing, and within minutes dozens of agitators began showing up. Those dozens soon turned into hundreds, and it wasn't long before the streets were teeming with more than three thousand militant gays yelling obscenities, blowing whistles, and coming within inches of our faces, screaming at

the top of their lungs. Soon the police, fearful of a major distur-
bance, arrived in force.

As the cacophony of noise, whistles, screams, and sirens
filled the air, the worship leader, and organizer of the outreach,
began to sing a very familiar refrain:

Oh, the blood of Jesus,
  Oh, the blood of Jesus,
Oh, the blood of Jesus,
  It washes white as snow.

We could barely hear him over the din, but soon scores of
praisers caught the chorus, and within seconds a wave swept
over us until all seven hundred of us were lifting our voices in
that one timeless chorus. *Oh, the blood of Jesus!* We must have
sung that for a half hour or more. Over and over again. What a
sight! What a contrast! Believers, surrounded by thousands of
militants, sweetly singing of the Savior's victory.

And so it went. Soon the crowds dispersed, and we finished
singing. But the contrast that day between light and darkness
marked all of us for a lifetime. We saw that worshiping God is
actually a key to effectively engaging in spiritual warfare.

The day after our praise gathering, two influential men from
San Francisco's gay community sought out one of the outreach
leaders and told him, "We just want you to know that you
Christians were the winners yesterday." It was their acknowl-
edgment that responding to anger with humility, to hatred with
love, had won the day.

In truth, the key to that victory was corporate worship, lifted up in the streets. For we saw Psalm 22:3 played out before our eyes: "You…inhabit the praises of [Your people]" (NKJV) or, as this verse can be read, "Where the Lord's people praise Him, there His authority is established." The worship of God had allowed His presence to envelop that piece of San Francisco real estate for that period of time, drawing hearts to Himself. Over the next several days many found new life in Christ and were baptized in the Pacific Ocean.

This episode underscores the synergistic relationship between worship and spiritual warfare. In Psalm 149:5–8 we read, "Let the saints rejoice in this honor and sing for joy on their beds. May the praise of God be in their mouths and a double-edged sword in their hands…to bind their kings with fetters, their nobles with shackles of iron." Though this Psalm is set in the context of an ancient military campaign, there is an application for us today.

The apostle Paul tells us in Ephesians 6 that we don't wrestle against flesh and blood, but against "principalities and powers" of darkness (see v. 12, NKJV). In this sense, I believe that the "kings and nobles" in Psalm 149 refer to those same principalities and powers that attempt to harass and harangue the saints. What is it, then, that binds the enemy, makes him ineffective, and neutralizes his power? We find the answer in verse 6, which tells us that our weapon is "the high praise of God…and the double-edged sword." We see here an allusion to the relationship between worship and spiritual warfare. As we praise Him and effectively bring the authority of Scripture to bear, the enemy is bound and rendered powerless. We see hints of this in Psalm 23, when David exults, "You prepare a table before me in the presence of my enemies" (v. 5). The table of fellowship with God—right in the midst of a battle!

One of the most striking illustrations of how praise and worship set the stage on which the Holy Spirit can rout demonic forces is the famous account of Jehoshaphat in 2 Chronicles 20. Jehoshaphat was a godly king who had done much to turn his countrymen back to the Lord. Later in his reign, a vast army from Edom came against him, prompting Jehoshaphat to proclaim a fast. As all the people sought the Lord, the Holy Spirit inspired one of the Levites to tell them, "You will not have to fight this battle. Take up your positions; stand firm and see the deliverance the LORD will give you" (v. 17). Early the next morning, Jehoshaphat appointed men to sing praise to the Lord as they went out at the head of the army: "Give thanks to the LORD, for his love endures forever" (v. 21). As they began to praise the Lord, He ambushed their enemies, inciting them to fight among themselves and annihilate each other. The act of praise became their strategic touchstone.

THE SYNERGY OF WORSHIP AND WARFARE

There is a dynamic connection between worship and effective spiritual warfare. To engage in prayer, or to resist the enemy, without adoring God through worship is to invite imbalance and ultimately spiritual discouragement. Our vision of God must loom larger than the specter of the enemy's attacks or the magnitude of our difficulties. The converse is true as well. If worship doesn't lead us to engage effectively in intercession and spiritual warfare, it may be because our worship has deteriorated into nothing more than a cathartic experience. Genuine worship will provoke us to pray.

We might say that worship is the *lungs of warfare,* and warfare the *fist of worship.* True spiritual worship has a focused violence about it. We adore a God whose order runs completely counter to a world system based on fear, anger, and pride.

So how do we define this relationship between worship and spiritual warfare? Although it is inappropriate to say that worship is an *instrument* of spiritual warfare, it is quite appropriate to discern that there *is* a scriptural relationship between the two.

Worship and praise sensitize us to the presence of the kingdom of God.

Remember, the "kingdom of God" really means Christ's rule. In other words, wherever Jesus is in charge, the kingdom of God is manifest. Again, in Psalm 22:3, we read that the Lord inhabits the praises of His people (NKJV). As we have seen, this passage can be better understood as "The Lord's rulership is realized wherever God's people praise Him." As we worship Him, Christ brings His rule to bear on specific situations. I have seen this again and again. The *adoration* of the Lord prepares us to yield to the *authority* of the Lord.

A few years ago I was teaching at a conference in Lyons, France. While there, I met an American missionary who had been living in France for a number of years. She recounted a fascinating story to me. Some years earlier I had written a worship musical titled *We Are Called*. A pastor friend of mine in the south of France translated the whole musical into French, put a choir together, and toured the country. Apparently it had brought widespread worship renewal to many areas.

This missionary had been part of the choir, and she told me that at the time two Muslim foreign exchange students were staying with her. She invited them repeatedly to the presentations of *We Are Called*, but each time they politely refused. One of the young ladies was what we might call a cultural Muslim, but the other was radical about her faith and wanted nothing to do with the gospel. Finally, though, they consented to attend the last performance. They figured that because of the missionary's hospitality, they owed it to her.

That evening was given over entirely to the worship of Jesus. No one preached or gave an altar call. Toward the climax of the musical, these two Islamic students were seized with wonder. It was as if the Father's arms swept them into His strong embrace. The radical Muslim said that she *actually saw Jesus,* standing in front of her! She fell to her knees and instantly gave her life to Christ. Both girls were soundly converted that night. Years later, they continued to risk their lives as they spread the gospel of Jesus in their homeland.

What had effected such a change in these women? Worship had "made room for the kingdom." In the atmosphere of worship, they felt the palpable presence of Jesus and were thus transformed.

Worship and praise often create the context in which God garners the firstfruits of the harvest.

We see this principle demonstrated in Acts 2, which contains the account of three thousand people being added to the church on that celebrated Pentecost day. Was this great "harvest" due to Peter's effective preaching alone? No, for Peter's inspired sermon came on the heels of an explosion of praise and worship. The Holy Spirit had filled the disciples, and they began to speak in other languages declaring the wonders of God. Those original believers simply worshiped God, and the curiosity of many was aroused. Peter's sermon was simply the net God used to bring in the catch.

Likewise, when Joshua took Jericho, he did it not by his military prowess, but by simply marching around the city walls in obedience to God's word. The Bible tells us that on that seventh day, when their march was complete, they lifted up a shout—no doubt a shout of praise to God's greatness—and the walls collapsed and victory was won (Joshua 6:12–21).

In both instances, a praising people was central to God's strategy of evangelism and warfare. There have been and always will be missions that call for detailed planning and conventional tactics. But at the outset, to both the apostles and Joshua, God seemed to be saying that fruitful evangelism and effective warfare are not a matter of the panache of our programs or of our skills, but of the release of His power. A lifestyle of worship serves to keep this truth ever before us.

Worship is an essential part of our preparation for spiritual warfare and evangelism.

For a number of years I had the privilege of leading youth mission teams in many areas around the world. On one such excursion, we ministered in a city of approximately seventy-five thousand in the southeastern part of the United States. We had planned on the first day of our outreach to simply fan out all over the city, praying two by two as we walked the neighborhoods and districts. Prior to this particular prayer walk, we gathered in a side room of a church sanctuary to spend time in worship.

That morning it seemed as though our voices were joined by a chorus of angels! Our singing intensified as we sought God for the city. All at once, one of the outreach leaders received a vivid impression in his mind. As we worshiped God, he saw a great hairy beast rise out of the middle of the city, then slowly back away into the ocean until he disappeared. We took that as a sign that God had heard our prayers and that He was going to do something significant in the city that day.

As we concluded our time of worship, we loaded into the vans and went to our designated neighborhoods. When we gathered later that evening, team after team reported an unusual sense that the power of God had broken through in that city.

Just how mightily God had broken through was demonstrated nine months later when the local host of the outreach called me. "You will never believe what has happened since your team was here!" he said excitedly. "In just the last few months, nine adult bookstores in our city have gone out of business, one adult movie theater has gone out of business, and one of the buildings that had housed an adult bookstore is now being used as a Christian bookstore!" We rejoiced together for what God had accomplished.

Results of such prayer walks aren't always this dramatic. But this experience underscored one principle: Preparing ourselves for ministry in worship allows the Holy Spirit to build faith in our hearts so that we can pray and minister—in short, do spiritual battle—more effectively.

Worshiping God distracts the enemy and frustrates his purpose.

In Ezekiel 28:11–19 we read one of the most detailed descriptions of Lucifer in Scripture. Though the prophet Ezekiel is addressing the king of Tyre in this passage, early in his diatribe he jumps from the temporal realm to the eternal: "You were in Eden, the garden of God" (v. 13). Clearly, the prophet is speaking not of the king of Tyre at this point but of Satan himself.

We can make some intriguing observations from this text. It seems that Lucifer was a guardian cherub ordained by God. It has been speculated that the position of guardian cherub refers to Lucifer's role as the archangel who guarded the glory of God. It has also been conjectured that as guardian of God's glory, Lucifer actually led the angelic hosts in the worship of God. In other words, what Gabriel was to the *word of God* and Michael was to the *power of God*, Lucifer was to the *glory of God*. It may be that because of this, Lucifer got closer than any other created being to God. Yet according to Isaiah 14, Satan's heart was infected with pride, wanting to become like God.

Ezekiel 28:13 is an intriguing passage. In the latter part of the verse, as Ezekiel is describing the physical appearance of Lucifer, the text says, "Your settings and mountings were made of gold." There is debate as to what this phrase actually means. Yet there is some indication that what is being described here is an unusual aspect of Lucifer's design. The Hebrew suggests that Lucifer was created in such a way that musical sounds emanated from his being.[1] Since Lucifer, meaning "light-bearer," was the guardian cherub, some speculate that he had something to do with actually enhancing the worship of the glory of God.

Basilea Schlink writes, "The power and greatness of this 'son of light' must have been beyond imagination. As the 'light-bearer' of God he would have manifested and reflected the divine glory and beauty in all their fullness."[2] Interesting thought. Yet Lucifer got so close to the worship of God that he finally wanted to taste that worship. Filled with jealousy and craving worship, Lucifer directed creation's focus on himself. Because of his treason, He was expelled from the mount of God and thrown to earth.

I believe that it's entirely possible that God is grooming a replacement for Lucifer. However, this time it will not be an archangel "guarding His glory"—it will be the corporate man, the bride of Christ, the church. By His grace, we are being prepared to be those who would usher in the worship of God for eternity!

Yet could it be that when God's people worship Him now, it somehow affects Satan and the evil he seeks to spew? Could it be that worship distracts the enemy and frustrates his demonic counsels? Imagine: The enemy and his minions have stratagems and blueprints they want to carry out against your city. Strategies against businesspeople, government leaders, artists, teachers, enslaving some to bitterness, ensnaring others with pride. But as the enemy attempts to carry out his schemes, he suddenly hears the sound of believer after believer, congregation after congregation, worshiping the Lord. Could it be that such sounds of worship actually remind Satan of what he has lost and will never have again? Could it be that those sounds of worship actually distract him and frustrate him from carrying out his purpose?

Perhaps this all sounds just too Gene Roddenberry to us. This seems the stuff of sci-fi novels, not thorough biblical exegesis. But…it could be. It certainly is interesting to reflect on such a possibility. One thing is certain: *If what Satan wants is the glory, then giving the glory to God is our ultimate expression of resistance against the enemy!*

Perhaps no other figure in Scripture combines worship and warfare like King David. The man after God's own heart was both devoted worshiper and consummate warrior. Some have suggested that David was the greatest missionary in the Old Testament.[3] Of course, he was no missionary in the conventional sense. But clearly, David understood the connection between the fervent worship of God and the model of goodness and prosperity that would attract the nations of the earth. In David's theology, he understood that to worship wholeheartedly was to yield to God's rulership, inviting His presence into one's world.

The Palestinian monks used a certain Greek word to describe "intimacy with God." The word was *parresia.* John

Binns, in his book *Ascetics and Ambassadors of Christ: The Monasteries of Palestine, 314–631 A.D.,* describes this term.

> In classical Greek, parresia was a political term which described the privilege, much prized in the city-states, of speaking openly. It could refer to the right to speak, or the quality of truth within the speech, or to the courage required to state convictions honestly. In the New Testament, parresia describes the confidence with which the gospel is proclaimed by the Apostles. They speak without fear of persecution, or any obstacle. So after Peter and John had been released from prison, the congregation prayed together and "all were filled with the Holy Spirit and spoke the word of God with par-resia—boldness" (Acts 4:31; see also Acts 2:29; 4:13; 9:27; 13:46; Ephesians 6:19; 1 Thessalonians 2:2).[4]

Let us never think that images of intimacy with God suggest passivity, withdrawal, or detached reflection. Though we can relish the marital motif and celebrate our place as His bride, we needn't overly feminize the idea in a manner that conveys docility. Intimacy with God does not mean being effete in the world. Intimacy with God has teeth to it—we not only dance with God, but also dance upon the serpent's head.

CHAPTER 12

The Radical Middle
of worship

Powerful worship that invites the presence of God draws seekers
rather than repels them. Genuine worship is evangelistic.

DOUG BANISTER

S ounds of celebration could be heard throughout the countryside. King David and his thousands had jubilantly proceeded for ten miles, dancing and singing to the music of lyres and trumpet blasts. The ark of the covenant was being brought to Jerusalem! When the ark entered the city, David could be seen dancing wildly before God, wearing only the white shoulder dress undergarment of the priest.

Standing at a window, David's first wife, Michal, watched as her husband exulted…and she loathed him. From her perspective, he had forgotten himself and was acting the fool. She could not understand how a man God had so exalted could now cavort like a commoner.

When David returned home, she scorned him, accusing him of crass vulgarity. David responded indignantly: "It was before the LORD, who chose me rather than your father or anyone…. I will celebrate before the LORD" (2 Samuel 6:21).

Because of Michal's pride, God humbled her, and she remained childless to the end of her days.

Most people conclude that David was the good guy in this story because he exhibited wholehearted worship before God and that Michal was the villain because she despised that which David offered in pure abandon. That is certainly a valid conclusion as the text clearly indicates that Michal was wrong in her response to David. But I suggest that there is a story behind the story.

I once heard Floyd McClung observe that this passage actually gives us a peek into a dysfunctional marriage and that David is not altogether guiltless in this particular situation.

For Michal was not always the aloof combatant she is portrayed as in this story. No, there was a time when Michal worshiped David, even lied to protect him. Caught in the politics of the royal family, she was forced to abandon David. Eventually, she married again.

When David became king, he decided that Michal still belonged to him. So in an act of privileged prerogative, he goes to fetch what was properly his—like a traveler claiming his baggage. The sorry picture of a monarch asserting his rights while husband number two can only sob inconsolably is pitiful. There is a noticeable lack of sensitivity on David's part. And as we read between the lines, I think we can see the seeds of distrust between David and Michael being sown.

Michal was clearly wrong for despising David as he danced before the Lord. Could it be that a pattern of insensitivity and poor communication on David's part contributed to Michal's disposition? Did David spend any time with Michal helping her understand what he was about to do? Was her attitude reflective not only of her arrogance, but also of David's failure to build bridges of understanding?

I think there is some timely application for us here. It is ironic that the most intimate expression of our relationship with God—our worship—is what seems to cause more friction in the church than almost anything else. Debates over worship styles and tension over appropriate worship behaviors have spawned much consternation and caused none too few congregational splits. There are valid questions concerning how we worship. Do we raise or clap our hands? Should celebratory movement—bodily gestures—be allowed in the church service? How expressive do we allow our corporate worship to get? When are our concerns for social protocol muted by our hunger for God's presence? And at what point does worship degenerate into self-serving emotionalism?

These questions cannot be answered fully in a chapter, but I think we can chart a basic road map that at least enables us to navigate between extremes and find what I call the "radical middle of worship." At the end of our journey, may we—unlike Michal—value that abandoned worship that God is so supremely worthy. And may we also—unlike David—seek to build bridges of understanding between the different clans in the body of Christ, as well as to honest seekers who genuinely hunger for God.

THE RADICAL MIDDLE: WORSHIP AND THE WORD

The word *balance* can strike some people as a code word for compromise. Calls for balance are sometimes expressions from those who are disconcerted by the new, the progressive, even the wild. This is especially true in the spiritual realm; history is replete with examples of spiritual zeal that deteriorated into excesses, thus creating manipulative and unbiblical environments. Such concerns are understandable, but the pursuit of balance was never meant to quench the flames of godly enthusiasm or mute the high praises of God.

Efforts at striking a balance in worship should not simply be attempts to determine spiritual protocols or subtly enforce stylistic preferences. Rather, these efforts should be the result of our applying the full counsel of the written Word to every facet of our worship experience.

Worship helps us digest the Word. In other words, when we receive truth from the Scriptures, responding in worship not only helps us focus on the truth we've received, but also enlarges our capacity to receive *more* truth. How can we maintain this balance between worship and the Word?

I'd like to put forth three principles that can ground our worship within healthy parameters:

Worship must be tethered to the Word.

The Father seeks worship that is expressed "in spirit and in truth" (John 4:24). When our worship becomes separated from truth, it rapidly deteriorates into religiosity, where experience itself becomes the barometer of our spirituality. This is nothing more than a deceptive spirituality that alleviates feelings of guilt but doesn't change character. There are four foundational truths that inform and shape our understanding of worship:

- the character of God,
- the lordship of Christ,
- the covenant of grace,
- the biblical vision of the church.

Apart from an understanding of God's character, worship is noise without substance. Apart from Christ's lordship, it is unbridled emotion and misguided zeal. Without comprehending God's covenant of grace, worship becomes another effort at working up a sense of emotional climax rather than joyfully responding to His presence. And without a biblical vision of the church worship, instead of fostering comradeship, degenerates into an imbalanced personal mysticism.

Worship, by its nature of opening us to an encounter with God, cultivates spiritual sensitivity.

We needn't balk here for fear of misguided emotionalism. Worship is neither a spiritual slot in our lives, nor a designated religious gathering. Worship is not a spectator sport, nor merely an emotional response. Worship is the means of divine communion, the dynamic that turns principles into lifestyle, the doorway to knowing God's presence in our lives. It is the secret to experiencing truth because it is the secret to encountering God, which is the fountainhead that both satisfies and whets our appetite for righteousness. Worship is the face-to-face of our relationship with God, the sum total of our communion with His Spirit, our reception of His life, and our responses to His revelation. Worship is a lifestyle.

Worship enables us to experience Christ's lordship, and thus it becomes a key to modeling His kingdom through the church.

Worship is the experiential hinge upon which the various facets of truth turn. Its exercise is essential for transforming our understanding of Christ's lordship from mere doctrine to daily submission. As we praise and worship Him, we are sensitized to the umpiring of His Spirit (Colossians 3:16)—His promptings, His warnings, His leadings, His comfort—which internalizes Christ's rule within us.

As believers walk *collectively* as disciples—most visibly in the local church—they model Christ's kingdom rule before the world, hence the relationship between a lifestyle of worship and the expression of the kingdom on earth. A community of such worshipers—those who allow Christ's rule to be exercised in the appropriate release of His gifts, who see the "Word made flesh" continuously—is an awesome force indeed. Modeling the kingdom corporately is the natural result of each person submitting to the kingdom individually. Praise and worship cultivate an appetite for the Word and sensitivity to His presence, thus synchronizing our desires and actions so that our lives are a constant ballet between obedience and blessing.

With Scripture as boundary, the primary pursuit of cultivating spiritual sensitivity and experiencing Christ's lordship as our singular aim serves to nudge us to that place of balance where worship can be offered both freely and appropriately.

THE RADICAL MIDDLE:
WORSHIP AND WORK

To live with the ultimate purpose of worshiping God and giving Him pleasure runs counter to popular culture. You can't quantify or itemize this purpose. It's a state of being, not doing, and we generally have a tough time with that.

By and large, our culture is task oriented—meaning we tend to measure our value by what we accomplish. This task orientation is actually a result of man's original rebellion in the Garden, and when we buy into it, we no less than perpetuate that perversion. We often mistakenly perceive worship as being a passive and unproductive endeavor because our mind is warped toward task orientation.

Adam rebelled because, among other reasons, he desired to control his own life. He attempted to assume a place of power and usurp an authority for which he wasn't designed. Because man wanted power, God fit the consequences to the crime: "By the sweat of your brow you will eat your food" (Genesis 3:19). Man wanted control, so God gave him over to it; thereby tasks became man's source of sustenance. He was to survive by what he did, not by to whom he was related.

Before the Fall, worship was not an unproductive activity but man's very wellspring of existence. For it was in that place of divine intercourse that man realized the continuous strength, wisdom, and motivation that enabled him to steward God's creation with joy. Far from being an occasional response to God, worship was man's very protection against the futility of a double mind. All this changed at the Fall. Man's thinking became twisted, his understanding reversed. Man began valuing his tasks and not his expression of character.

This is in part why it is difficult for us to value a lifestyle of worship today. We want to worship God, but we are constantly sucked back into a maelstrom of busyness that somehow justifies our existence. Some actually *fear* a lifestyle of worship, thinking that it may blunt their drive to succeed. And this may be true in part, for the tension between results and relationship still wars within us.

In our attempt to bridge the gap between works and worship, we in effect relegate worship to a category of works. So we are ever torn between worship—adoring, obeying, and enjoying the Father—and trying to be productive. And here is our fatal mistake, for by attempting to strike this balance *ourselves,* we unknowingly partake of the forbidden fruit all over again. In this place of control, we repeatedly flirt with God's curse.

Before man rebelled, he did not have to balance worship and work—worship was the balance. Before the Fall, work flowed out of worship. We need to return to this sequence. We are not to balance being and doing, worship and work, and relationship and results—rather the latter should flow from the former.

We are addicted to the consequences of our sin, and it takes a radical withdrawal to come to a place where worship is our lifestyle and work the overflow. For the apostle Paul, it meant three years of solitude in an Arabian desert. The vast majority of us will never be in a place like that, but we can instead purpose in our hearts to abandon our self-serving goals, our expectations, our drive for recognition and success, and our need for approval and esteem…and discover God! For many of us, this kind of reorientation of our values may require us to go into a kind of desert. For only then can we put our focus solely on God Himself.

Once we finally center our devotion on God and live in that continual response of worship, we will discover those goals, expectations, and drives that are the offspring of that divine intercourse to which we've abandoned ourselves. That kind of productivity is the natural child of divine love, which is a walk of peace not pressure, of joy not anxiety.

THE RADICAL MIDDLE: WORSHIP OF GOD AND NEEDS OF PEOPLE

Leonard Sweet, an articulate analyst of postmodern culture, comments:

> Post moderns exhibit three levels of engagement with media [with life itself?], according to Myra Stark [senior vice president with the advertising giant Saatchi and Saatchi]: "fascination, exploration, integration." Post moderns have to explore [hands on] before they can integrate. Of these three stages, only the first is passive [fascination]. Both exploration and integration are active and interactive.[1]

The three needs to which Sweet refers—fascination, exploration, and integration—are as critical to address in our worship styles as they are in any other aspect of life. One of the reasons worship has been such a focus in the church in recent years is that believers have a growing hunger to *experience* God. This hunger is fed, in part, by those three needs.

Fascination

The appetite for something higher than the daily humdrum is enormous throughout our culture. The increased interest in angels over the last several years is but a small sampling of the deep need registering in many for the "otherworldly."

At a time when many churches seek to be culturally relevant by tailoring the gospel to the lowest common denominator of human want, the honest truth seeker wants his or her taste of spirituality to *feel* spiritual. Whether or not they know it, what they want is a sense of transcendence.

Exploration

Too many believers are beginning to see Christianity as no longer fresh. They may desire to remain orthodox but are no longer satisfied with "cranial Christianity"—sound exegesis that is not necessarily supported by obvious signs of God's supernatural intervention in their lives. Many Christians want to explore how their relationship with God impacts the warp and woof of their existence, to experience a convergence between solid biblical teaching and genuine spiritual encounter. They have been searching for that missing jewel and have rediscovered the joy of simply adoring God. But at the same time, they want to be anchored to the unchanging standard of Scripture so they can be confident that what they are encountering is integral to the biblical record.

Integration between truth and practice

How is truth discovered? What process filters information about spiritual things into our experience? What translates knowledge into wisdom and right thinking into right living? To the media children, those who have left behind the more linear thought patterns of their parents and who thrive on the visual and experiential, these questions demand fresh answers.

It is not enough for us to understand God's covenant of grace; we are to joy in it! It is not enough to discuss our need to be a covenant community; we need to *want* to be a covenant community. The act of worship brings pleasure to the heart of God, who then by His Spirit creates within us the *desire* to apply truth.

Worship is the point of balance in all of life because it meshes life's facets into one focus: the Lord. It is wise not to focus on balance itself. Rarely do we work at balancing ourselves as we walk throughout the day. We simply walk, and balance is the by-product of being healthy. A high-wire acrobat knows that when he tiptoes across the wire, he does not look at his feet in order to stay balanced. He looks straight ahead.

Unfortunately, the church has endured much division over the issue of worship. Personal styles and preferences have all too often become barriers to unity. Fixing our eyes on Jesus not only keeps us balanced, but also engenders an inward "poise of the heart"—that posture of humility that enables us to persistently reach for unity.

CHAPTER 13

A Dwelling place for His presence

Religion is what happens when the Holy Spirit leaves the house.
BONO, LEAD SINGER OF U2

I sat in the studio, listening to the tracks of a worship song I'd written years before.

Jesus, all-glorious, create in us a temple
        Called as living stones where You're enthroned…

As the orchestra swelled to a crescendo and the choir began singing the chorus, my eyes glistened with tears:

O the glory of Your Presence
        We Your temple give You reverence
Come and rise to Your rest and be blessed by our praise
        As we glory in Your embrace
As Your Presence now fills this place.[1]

The glory of His presence! The magnificence of all that He is, sweeping over our souls in wave after wave of unbounded joy.
The glory of His presence! I knew that walking with God was

more than reading about Him in His Word or listening to a sermon. To walk with God is to encounter Him, to become *aware*
of His nearness.

The glory of His presence! A place where the Scriptures burn
in the heart, where the soul is drawn out of its voracious self-
absorption into a fascination with His holiness, where a person
can sense the reality of His presence just as surely as if his best
friend entered the room.

No wonder David invited us to "taste and see that the Lord
is good" (Psalm 34:8). There is a spiritual faculty of perception
that functions at a deeper level than the mercurial cadence of
mere human emotion. God can be *tasted,* if you will, encountered. David's supreme quest was to gaze on the beauty of the
Lord. We can become aware of His beauty as sure as we can be
captivated by a fiery sunset or a rose in full bloom. For God created us to *experience* Him.

My attempt to capture this truth led me to pen this chorus.
It expressed not only my hunger for His presence, but also my
passion for His abiding glory. The biblical account of God's glory
filling Solomon's temple fascinated me (2 Chronicles 6–8).
Could God's glorious presence dwell in a place? I wondered. Of
course I knew that God is omnipresent, and that as Stephen
said, no edifice of men can contain Him (see Acts 7:48–50). But
Stephen went on to convey the idea that God wants to make *His
habitation* in a people. So He graced and sanctioned Solomon's
temple for that purpose—to give us a picture of His desire to
localize His manifestation.

This idea that God wants to uniquely manifest His presence

in specific situations made sense to me. As I reflected on my spiritual journey, I recalled those occasions when I sensed the beauty of God's presence in overwhelming ways—when I was with certain congregations, or during an especially rich worship gathering. Times when I felt, in the words of David McCullough, "the consuming fire of holiness [which] is a bonfire of love set to burning against the world's night."[2]

Were such feelings but trifling emotion? Or an attempt to effect a cathartic moment in order to reassure myself that God exists? Or zeal looking for release?

Or could one spiritually discern that moment when God touches the human spirit? Was there a difference between the truth of God's gracious, "ever-present help" (Psalm 46:1) and the *manifestation* of His presence? Between the indwelling Spirit and the palpable "weight" of His glory all around me? And if there was a difference, was there anything I could do to make way in my heart for Him to reveal that glory, that way David pined for when he desired to "gaze upon the beauty of the LORD" (Psalm 27:4)?

Of course, I understood the danger of seeking spiritual experience instead of the Lord Himself and had resolved not to fall into that trap. Still, I knew that relationship with God was more than mental assent to a set of creeds, more than faith devoid of joy. I wanted a "faith-to-face" relationship with God.

In Solomon's day, God's glory came to a temple. That was but a foreshadowing of another temple—a temple made not by human hands but formed with the hearts of those who love Christ. The apostle Paul speaks of us as a holy temple, "fitly framed together" (Ephesians 2:20–22, KJV). The apostle Peter, likewise, calls us living stones that are being built into a spiritual house (1 Peter 2:5).

This temple, too, is to be filled with His glory. And this temple imagery reminds us that worship is not simply individual communion with God, but a corporate expression to God. It reminds us that the flame of holy passion is rekindled not only in our personal pursuit of divine intimacy, but also in our commitment to rightly relate to one another as believers.

God's love had conquered me, and I wanted Him to be revealed before everyone. But seeing the people of God as a holy temple in which He manifests His glory helped me recognize my responsibilities to my brothers and sisters. It helped me focus on those attitudes and actions that make me the kind of stone that can be "fitly framed" into His temple—for only as we are built together will the world see the fullness of Christ's glory. To worship God without concerning ourselves with how we relate to His people will eventually result in a highly privatized spirituality, which can render us vulnerable to deception.

Therefore, we need to ask ourselves how we can be fitly framed together.

FITTING TOGETHER GOD'S WAY

Centuries after Solomon dedicated the first temple, it was destroyed and the people were carted off to Babylon where they languished in captivity for seventy years. At the end of this time, a vanguard of Jews, under Zerubbabel, was allowed to return to Jerusalem and rebuild the temple. Exploring the rebuilding of

Solomon's temple sketches for us a useful template that can help us understand what it means to be fitly framed together. For as it was with that temple, so it is with us: As we are built together to become His holy habitation, the world will see His glory.

The book of Ezra records the rebuilding program, which reached a high-water mark when the temple's foundation was laid. This aroused fierce opposition from the Jews' enemies, and construction eventually came to a halt. In a matter of time two prophets, Haggai and Zechariah, stirred Zerubbabel and the people to finish the task. Haggai strongly rebuked the nation for neglecting "God's habitation" in favor of her own comforts. The account of the second temple's construction, along with Haggai's sermon, which is recorded in the first chapter of his book, gives us patterns to follow and principles to apply as we allow the Spirit to build us into a "spiritual temple" in which Christ is manifest and His glory revealed.

First, opposition did not arise when they were laying foundations. It commenced when they started building.
In the book of Ezra, we read that it was *after* the Jews laid the temple's foundation that their enemies saw them join "stone to stone" and were angered.

Foundation times are hidden times, times to focus on basics, times when plans are fresh and vision runs high. Whether it's the predictable honeymoon period in a new presidential administration, the birth of a new church, or even the baby steps of a person's newfound relationship with Christ, foundations are times of rediscovered identity, times of focusing on one's individual promise and potential.

It is when the Holy Spirit begins to join us stone to stone that the enemy seeks to jump us. Being joined stone to stone—being connected relationally—is paramount if we want the composite of our gifts to reflect the beauty of Jesus. For Christ's beauty is only fully displayed when each one's gift is interlaid into the mosaic of His image.

That is why it is at the point of our relationships that Satan targets his assaults. We see other people's faults, become testy when provoked by another's idiosyncratic behavior, and experience one too many conflicts with others. We begin to think it too exasperating to forbear one another, too hard to keep forgiving one another, too difficult to love one another. After a while, we say to ourselves, *I don't need this! Building relationships is just too difficult.*

Yet being aware of Satan's strategy of targeting us at this point in our relationships gives us a leg up in our efforts to maintain them.

Second, they had a command to build; therefore, opposition was to be broken by obedience.

When Haggai begins preaching to the Israelites, he declares "This is what the LORD Almighty says: 'These people say, "The time has not yet come for the LORD's house to be built"'" (Haggai 1:2). The people had taken false refuge in a misperception of God's sovereignty. To them, opposition meant that God was not blessing their efforts. But God did not want them to measure their endeavors by circumstances. He had given them a word, and they were to obey at all costs. They were not to allow their adverse circumstances to write the script.

Calls to obedience can sometimes come off as so much same ol', same ol', and we can forget the power that is released when we obey God's commands. Something of an atomic reaction is unleashed in one simple act of obedience, a reaction that can eventually affect thousands.

In Romans 5:19 we read, "Just as through the disobedience of the one man the many were made sinners, so also through the obedience of the one man the many will be made righteous." Though this verse speaks exclusively of Christ's sacrificial work on our behalf, we can yet draw from it an encouraging application.

Years ago, I received a letter from a colleague, gently rebuking me for certain character flaws, flaws that were obviously compromising my behavior. I bristled when I read the letter. *Who does he think he is?* But within moments, I saw the wisdom in his admonition and yielded to the Spirit's conviction.

Later that day, I found myself in an impromptu counseling session with a missionary from Mexico. This leader had broad influence over thousands of people but had sustained considerable wear and was on the verge of leaving the ministry for good. During our conversation, wisdom poured out of me like a torrent from a broken dam. It was astonishing! And it was a watershed moment for that missionary.

Later as I prayed, I remarked to the Lord how unusual it was for me to dispense wisdom at *that* level, and He quickly reminded me that it had nothing to do with any keen perception on my part. It was, in fact, the result of a chain of obedience that began with my friend's letter and continued as I acquiesced to its rebukes. Obedience had provided a clear channel through which

God's wisdom could flow. Today that same missionary is touching millions around the world. Let us never minimize the importance of unseen acts of obedience—to pray when washing the dishes, to encourage someone who may seem unlovable, to hold our tongue when provoked. For though we may never see it this side of heaven, our obedience, catalyzed by divine grace, will bring many to Jesus.

Third, we often retreat to the safety of our own worlds when "building the temple" gets too hard.

Haggai goes on to say, "Is it a time for you yourselves to be living in your paneled houses, while this house remains a ruin?" (1:4). Fitting living stones rightly together is a long, tedious, arduous business. Over extended periods of time, it can also be largely unfulfilling. But we have to stay at it because a building—even a living building—is of little value until it is completed.

Still, we can come to the place where we just back away from our building commitments and withdraw into our own worlds—our hobbies, our work, even our families. We cease to cultivate in the body of Christ a sense of moving together as one man (Ephesians 4:13, NKJV).

The *house* for each of us is the relationships in the body of Christ to which God has connected us—our local church, our Bible study, our mission team. God calls us to be faithful in these relationships because the glory of His presence cannot be fully revealed through just one believer. He wants to express so much of Himself that it takes many to accomplish it. But those many must walk in the unity for which Christ prayed in John 17:21—

"that all of them may be one." It is the same unity the psalmist celebrated when he extolled, "How good and pleasant it is when brothers live together in unity!... For there the LORD bestows his blessing, even life forevermore" (Psalm 133:1, 3). That "life" is God's presence, for there is no other life apart from His presence. It is then as we maintain the unity in the bond of peace (Ephesians 4:3) that we know the fullness of His presence.

These are nice platitudes on paper. But when someone falsely accuses us, when someone's agenda collides with ours, when someone's temperament grates on us and we find ourselves locked in a tedious process of reconciliation—that's when our commitment to His temple is tested.

If I really want the world to see His glory, then I will do whatever I must to allow the Master Builder to rightly fit me into His temple—including tending to relationships, even at the cost of great inconvenience to me. And sometimes that inconvenience is working at a relationship that I would rather discard. The leader of a revolutionary movement once commented on why his organization was so strong. "I can always fall out with my comrade," he said, "but my brother is always my brother."[3]

I believe that God allows opposition in order to get us back to the issue of building relationships, and to remind us that we don't build relationships for a payoff but because it is the right thing to do. We must steward our relationships, with all the bumps along the way, *not* because it makes us more productive but because it is right.

We Americans are highly results oriented. We can get very impatient when we don't see some measurable yield from our investments. I believe that God allows a fair amount of relational conflict within the American church in order to wean us from our addiction to productivity. Ironic as it seems, perhaps God allows friction in relationships so that we might recover our prophetic edge: *Doing things simply because it is right, not for personal advantage.*

The bottom line is this: If we have a heart for God's revealed glory, we'll have a heart for His temple and thus stay tethered to one another.

Fourth, neglecting His temple results in deep dissatisfaction.

Haggai 1:5–6 accurately describes many in the church: We plant much but harvest little, eat but never have enough, and drink but never have our fill. When we don't give proper attention to the temple of God—when we don't allow the Holy Spirit to rightly fit us together in covenant relationships for the sake of Christ's glory—we will find ourselves indulging in a not-enough attitude. This in turn incubates feelings of dissatisfaction, restlessness, disappointment.

Fifth, the strength of God's rebuke is proportionate to the glory of our destiny in Him.

The rebuke recorded in Haggai 1:7–11 is a shocking one. It speaks of judgment on the fruit of their hands, judgment on their livestock, judgment on their homes. Such severe discipline is especially mind numbing when you consider that these returning captives had a heart for God and had already labored diligently. In fact, when we read Ezra's account, we find that the people didn't just turn over and quit at the earliest sign of hostility; they kept at it until a concerted effort on the part of their enemies forced them to shut down.

Still God does not mince words; He rebukes them sternly. I think God's rebuke was so severe because He saw that His people were in danger of missing their destiny. God was accelerating His program in order to prepare all things for the coming of His Son, and this rebuke was His way of bearing down on the people in order to rescue them from their stupor and propel them into their glorious future.

If we love God, we'll do whatever it takes for Jesus to be seen. And if we want Jesus to be seen, our supreme desire will be to be rightly fitted in His temple.

A TEMPLE FOR HIS DWELLING

What practical steps can we take to cultivate hearts that are committed to one another? How can we nurture attitudes of commitment to establishing a dwelling place for God's glory?

I would like to suggest the following steps:

Let Jesus, the Master Builder, shape and polish us individually.

In Solomon's day, the stones for the temple were cut, shaped, and polished in the quarry from which they were dug, then carted up the mount and fitted together without the sound of a hammer.

Often, we neglect to allow the Master Builder to sufficiently cut, shape, and polish us. Consequently, when we try to fit, especially as we engage in ministry, we rub against each other and unnecessary conflict ensues. Attitudes like opportunism, jealousy, and personal ambition make it more difficult for us to fit with one another, so the world sees and hears a lot of hammering done in public—division, schism, and competition—and is often turned off by the church and thus disregards our message.

To be rightly fitted means that we will have to be refined in areas that normally wouldn't have to be touched if we were stones left to ourselves. This might border on the ingenuous, but imagine that you are a raw stone in the quarry. You are unique. You have your own unique shape with various edges of your "self" jutting out here and there, your rugged features rather beautiful in an unvarnished way. But then the builder selects you to fit into His temple. That means that some of those "unique edges" have to be chipped away, then polished. And God often smoothes us through relational conflict.

What a wonderful thing it is to allow the Master Builder to chisel and sand our character so that He can fit us together "without the sound of a hammer."

Allow God to put us where we fit best.
Once the stone was cut, smoothed, and polished, it had to be moved to another location—from the quarry to the mount—in order to be set in the temple.

This seems obvious, but the application is incisive: Sometimes we need to be willing to work outside our preferences. Our reluctance or refusal to do things outside of our predispositions, desires, and comfort zones can be a real hindrance to our fitting rightly together. For example, when someone in leadership asks us to do something we don't feel enthused about, it is easy to couch our apathy in terms of "God's leading" and resist arenas of service that don't emotionally fuel us. Being rightly fitted together often means dying to our own preferences.

We must humble ourselves and not seek to parade our abilities.

Being rightly fitted together means giving up some measure of exposure for the greater good of God's glory. Imagine that you are the first stone laid upon the next row of stones. At first, that seems pretty cool. After all, you're on top of the other stones. All of your sides are displayed for everyone to see except for the one side connected to the row beneath you. Then the Master Builder places another stone on one side of you, then another on the other side. *That's not so bad*, you think. *I still have three sides showing.* But then the Master Builder comes along and puts a stone on top. Now, only two of your six facets show.

Sometimes being rightly fitted means humbling ourselves and giving up the "right" to be noticed, to have our gifts or talents showcased. Jealousy, envy, and competition actually reveal a lack of love for God. If we love Him, we will long for His presence, and if we long for His presence, we will want His dwelling place to be established—with us fitting where He wants us to fit.

Remember that we have no say in where we are placed.

Just as the stones used to build the temple had no say about where they were placed, we must yield to God's wisdom as to where He places us in His temple. If it were up to me, I would want my stone set at eye level so all the passersby could see. I wouldn't want my stone placed near the foundation where someone had to stoop down to see it, or at the top of the wall, too high for anybody to see it. But we must have faith that the Master Builder knows exactly where to place us. We must lay aside our personal ambition and our desire to be noticed—by leadership or by anyone else—and be ready to go where Jesus sends us and do what He tells us to do.

The desire to be noticed and valued runs deep within us. Often, I have had people complaining to me, "My pastor doesn't recognize my gifts." How are we to respond when we are disregarded? In Matthew 20:20–28, Jesus opens a window for our souls: the call to servanthood.

Messages on servanthood don't usually evoke much enthusiasm in us. That may be because we haven't seen how close servanthood is to the heart of Jesus. "Whoever wants to become great," the Master said, "must be your servant" (20:26). Servanthood is at the heart of what Jesus came to earth to demonstrate. The apostle Paul wrote of this humility: "Who [Christ], being in very nature God, did not consider equality with God something to be grasped, but made himself nothing, taking the very nature of a servant…he humbled himself and became obedient to death—even death on a cross!" (Philippians 2:6–8).

Jesus can only affirm in us what is of Himself. He came not first as a prophet, though He is the acme of prophetic ministry. He came not first as a shepherd, though He is the chief. He was a provocateur, a healer, even a radical—He was all these things, but He expressed them only when servanthood demanded them. He was first and foremost a servant to His Father.

When we walk as servants, we are closest to the heart of Jesus. As we embrace servanthood, we know His affirmation and recognition at levels deeper than we have ever known, because we will find ourselves resonating with the depth of His call.

Our appetite for the glory of the Lord's presence is measured by how willing we are to let Him chisel, polish, and fit us into His house. It's wonderful when we are caught up in the ecstasy of song, when our hearts touch heaven even for a moment. But the intensity of our heart for Jesus registers in the intensity of our commitment to one another. This is worship at its purest, for it burns the self out of each of us. As George MacDonald once said, "To love our brother is to worship the consuming fire."[4]

a passion for His glory

Is this not our trouble, my dear friends, that we talk about God
and we believe in God, but we do not know God, the glory of God?

D. MARTIN LLOYD-JONES

My father has bequeathed to me perhaps one of the most important legacies a dad could leave his son: an insatiable hunger for the presence of God.

I was a sophomore in high school when my dad took a small pastorate in San Jose, California. Over the next few years, our little church enjoyed quite a renewal. People started attending from miles around. Soon, our "little" church was not so little anymore.

People were attracted to our church because they sensed the presence of the Lord at our gatherings. One of the reasons people felt God's presence was that Dad put a premium on both *giving* God glory and *experiencing* God's glory. A telling incident early in his pastorate demonstrates just how serious Dad was about the glory of the Lord. I'll let him put it in his own words:

I had been pastoring this church for about three years when we decided to throw an extravagant Christmas party for the entire church. By now the little flock of 100 had grown to 400 or so, but we were still small enough to enjoy a holiday bash at a beautiful lodge in the Santa Cruz Mountains. I had nothing to do with planning the party; I had left that entirely to my staff.

The night of the party was a jovial one indeed. One of the pastors dressed up as Santa Claus and gave out gag gifts, one of the other staff members led us all in singing "Winter Wonderland," "Silver Bells," and many other favorite Christmas songs. There was great food and a lot of laughs. But as the evening went on, my spirit became heavier. Finally towards the close of the evening, they gave it to me to wrap it up. I only had a few minutes to make a few remarks and close with "Silent Night." The church people had enjoyed themselves—but there was a heaviness in my heart.

On the drive home, I said to my wife Peggy that I had felt something had gone wrong. I didn't know exactly what it was, for it had been a wonderful night of fellowship. It was midnight when we got home, but I couldn't sleep. I began to pace back and forth in my family room crying out to God, and as I did, it began to dawn on me where we had erred. All I could say in prayer was, "We didn't glorify God, we didn't glorify God!" It had been a nice evening, a comfortable evening, but we had failed to truly give the Lord Jesus Christ center place. As I confessed this omission before the Lord, I began to feel the heaviness lift. But something still wasn't quite right. In times past, when I would have such encounters with the Lord, I would have confessed the sin and simply put it behind me.

But this time I felt the Holy Spirit tell me that it would not be enough. I actually felt myself consumed with a kind of panic—the great fear that we might lose that precious sense of the presence of God which had so marked our gatherings for the three years I had been there. It was not that I felt that the spirit of God was so touchy that the slightest missed step would offend him. Rather, it was the feeling that we had been given a treasure—the manifest presence of God—that I didn't want to lose! So intent was I that we do all we could to maintain the sense of his presence, that I called the entire pastoral staff over to my home at 3:00 in the morning to jointly confess what we had done. I'll never forget it—in the wee hours of Sunday morning the pastoral leadership on their faces, crying out to God not to withdraw his presence because we had simply neglected to glorify him at a Christmas party.

Sound extreme? Not when you have tasted sweet communion with the Lord. Not when you have come to the end of yourself, overwhelmed by your sense of inability, only to find that the great secret of any real success is the manifestation of his glory.[1]

At Home in His Glory

I ache to go home when ministry takes me away from my family. The last hour of my return flight can seem excruciatingly long. I can feel my wife's warm hug as I step off the plane; hear my daughters' voices chiming, "Daddy!"; see my son's broad grin when he meets me at baggage claim. Closing my eyes, I can

see myself settling into my favorite chair in my cozy study, nib-
bling on some of Nancy's fresh-baked brownies as I pass the
time working on a crossword puzzle. Oh, that last hour ticks
away so very slowly! But when I land, a bubble of peace seems
to envelop me.

All is right with the world. I am home.

We are spiritual beings, you and I. And we were made for a
home that cannot be built with human hands out of earthly
stuff. The pursuits of this world cannot satisfy us. We were
made to live in God's presence, to sense His whisperings, to
catch His heart, to gaze in awe at His glory.

This is the hunger that cannot be sated, the thirst that cannot be quenched—except by God Himself.

Our hunger for God's glory runs deep but often goes undis-
cerned. The need to be connected to a purpose larger than ourselves, the knowledge that wonder hovers all around us, the
yearning to nestle in arms of love, the jaunty pursuit of adventure—all these are but little inklings of that deeper desire to
touch and be touched by heaven.

The longing for God's glory is the ache to be home.

What is His glory? It is the sound of pure pleasure that the
Father, Son, and Holy Spirit enjoy. It is the perfect symphony of
every good attribute. Like the sun's rays blinding our eyes, it is
that moment when the light of who God is penetrates our darkness and fills our vision. It is all that He is—*made manifest.* His
glory is the atmosphere created by His character.

We long for righteousness, peace, and joy (see Romans
14:17), but these blessings come only in God's presence. When
we long for rest, we actually long for His glory. When we yearn

for adventure, we actually yearn for His glory. And while we can rest in the assurance that He will never leave us nor forsake us, there is yet a dimension of which the Puritans spoke when they looked for what they called God's manifest presence.

Understanding God's manifest presence means understanding the difference between *knowing* He is in the house and *encountering* Him in the house. I can know that my wife, Nancy, is in our home on a given afternoon. But if she's upstairs and I'm in the basement, I can't meet with her, talk with her, or enjoy her company. Of course, I am content to know that she is there.

My father's appetite for the glory of the Lord is but the continuation of a stream that has run throughout history, coursing through the hearts of saints through the ages, a stream that winds back all the way to Moses and beyond.

THE PROVOCATION TO GLORY

It had been a long, long journey for this melancholy man, Moses. As he sat on a stone outcropping perched high on a mountain overlooking the desert floor, all he could hear was the wind whistling through the rocky crevasses surrounding him. He was exhilarated, yet disappointed. He was satisfied, yet felt alone. He sat there reflecting on the lifetimes that seemed to be compressed into but a few short months.

He recalled the not-too-distant days when he had been cushioned in the security of anonymity. Thoughts of royal palaces seemed so distant then. Minding his sheep in the solace of the desert, he had lost track of the years. He'd found a new life, forged a new beginning. And then…that one bush! A bush with fiery leaves that inflamed his soul with a desire to know God and fulfill his destiny.

Wary though Moses was, he had made his way to Egypt. Watched God humble the mightiest force on earth. Nursed a million slaves as God molded them into a new nation. And witnessed miracles that defied even the stuff of myth and legend. He had seen a mountain explode in divine fire, heard the trumpet blasts of heaven, and received the greatest blueprint for society ever given to mankind.

And now here he was—shepherd, deliverer, leader, lawgiver, all at once. And he sat…and wondered.

All of this, only to be stunned by a disappointment he could not have anticipated. What was going to happen because of what had transpired the past few hours? He turned the recent events over in his mind again.

He'd been face-to-face with God as He etched His commands in tablets of stone. But as Moses descended the mount with the tablets, he heard a sound, a sound of song, a sound of celebration. It was a song his aid Joshua construed as the sound of war, but it was the sound of neither defeat nor victory. Suddenly a shadow came over Moses' face. His heart was seized with the ache of impending loss, with the realization that something pure had been stained, something precious stolen. Moses knew it was the sound of play. And as they descended down the mount farther, the orgy that filled his vision stunned him to his core.

Moses was ready for anything—or so he thought. He had steeled himself against Pharaoh's challenge, had embraced the hardships of a wilderness trek, had prepared himself for Sinai's fire. But he was not prepared for this. This was a people that had seen miracles beyond what any other generation had seen, a people that had been delivered from the mightiest power in the earth, a people God had miraculously sustained at the "bitter waters" (Exodus 15:22–27). Yet they had risen up to play, abandoning *Yahweh* in a moment.

Now, alone once again, Moses ascended the mount to plead his people's case with God. The miracles, the disappointments, the promises yet unfulfilled—suddenly all of these things grew very dim in his mind. For a moment he was transported beyond his disappointments, beyond his responsibilities. Now it was not a matter of reconciling himself to a disappointment, nor a matter of leading a million souls across the desert. All at once, the clamor of these voices grew faint, and he was enraptured by an impulse that seemed to emanate from the very depth of his being. Who he was and what he did no longer mattered. What he would or would not achieve suddenly became irrelevant. As if caught up in the deafening roar of angelic wings beating, Moses cried out to his God, "Show me your glory!" (Exodus 33:18).

Show me your glory! Whether articulated with great eloquence or sighed with groanings that cannot be put into words, this cry has been the core passion of God's children since the Garden. It is the cry of one who has become convinced that nothing else—no accomplishment, no relationship, not even the seizing of one's purpose and destiny—can possibly satisfy. Trying to find one's reason for being apart from God can be such an illusion because it promises so much yet satisfies so little.

And what had propelled Moses to this point? Was it some surprising revelation? Was it the discovery of some secret mystery? Was it the encounter with the divine power, which had opened the sea and then destroyed Egypt's army? Was it even the sense of being overwhelmed at the sheer presence of the Almighty as he stood face-to-face with Him, hearing Him thunder, "I Am that I Am"?

No. In fact, the entrance to this "dwelling place" had been none of these things. Instead, the pathway to God's glory began with *disappointment with God's people.*

As Moses' time on the mount drew to a close, God somberly informed him that his people had corrupted themselves. Upon his descent, Moses heard a sound. It was the sound of play. The people were neither overcoming in God, nor being overcome by Satan. Better to have been one or the other. For when we are defeated, we recognize our need, and when we are victorious, we recognize our God. But when we are at play, we recognize neither God nor our need. And that is the most dangerous place of all.

Faced with an uncertain future, troublesome terrain, enemies that they knew were there but could not see, a leader absent far longer than they had anticipated—*and* faced with a God displaying the fullness of His power and summoning them to covenant—the people rose up to play! Why, in the face of such restiveness, did they play? Because they did not worship.

Remember, Moses had demanded that Pharaoh let God's people go that they might simply go into the wilderness on a three-day's journey to *worship* the Lord. All that was necessary to overcome the uncertainty caused by the long delay in Moses' return and the challenges of the desert was the simple worship of the Lord.

At this point, God wasn't asking them to fight an enemy or implement a strategy. God wasn't asking them to take Jericho…yet. He simply wanted them to worship. But they did not. They amused themselves. They looked back to Egypt and found safe images—and they reduced their vision of the great I AM to one that fit their inclinations.

THE PATHWAY TO GOD'S GLORY

Ironically, Moses' response to his disappointment with them would determine whether they would realize their destiny. How was he going to respond? On this question, a nation hung in the balance. Yet, this was the beginning of Moses' journey to glory, and to reach that place he had to cross several thresholds.

The threshold of self-seeking

The first threshold Moses faced on his path to the secret place of the Most High was the threshold of self-seeking, which appeared before him as a grand doorway into a promising future—self-seeking masked as vision.

In Exodus 32:9–10, God makes Moses quite an offer: "'I have seen these people,' the LORD said to Moses, 'and they are a stiff-necked people. Now leave me alone so that my anger may burn against them and that I may destroy them. Then I will make you into a great nation.'"

God made Moses one of the greatest offers ever made: to be the progenitor of an entire nation. Moses could have taken great satisfaction in the fact that God obviously saw in him the faith-fulness, the skills, and the composite of character and giftings that would prompt Him to make such an offer. Affirmation from heaven is a heady brew indeed! When one receives the applause of God, he has realized the sum and substance of happi-ness…almost.

When people have disappointed us, it is easy to retreat to our giftings, to draw satisfaction from our potential. A pastor resigns because he is not appreciated; a leader withdraws to his preaching; a layperson disengages from improving his world and fritters away his time on his hobbies. How easy it is to say, "If I can't maximize my potential here, I'll go elsewhere."

Moses could have easily responded in this manner—and been justified in doing so. But he quickly rejects God's offer. He rejects the offer because he is more concerned with God's repu-tation than with his own potential. The basis of his decision was "What will get God the most glory?" not "How can I be ful-filled?" The pathway to God's glory inevitably leads us to this showdown with ourselves, as we ask ourselves this vital ques-tion: *Is my motivation to glorify God, even if it does not seem to mesh with my ideas about how my gifts and potential are best used?*

The pathway to God's glory means abandoning our desire to be admired and esteemed. If we are to know that place of His glory, then we must walk away from our future and our possi-bilities, even if it means embracing obscurity.

The threshold of bitterness

In Exodus 32:19–20 we find Moses responding in a fit of frus-tration to the orgy before him. Understandable. Yet in his rage, he throws down the tablets that God Himself had chiseled with His own finger. This was also understandable, but it was unauthorized.

This second threshold Moses had to pass was that of bitterness. Moses had sacrificed beyond measure, but for what? A people who played around at the earliest opportunity. But in momentarily succumbing to bitterness, Moses destroyed what God had done. Later, Moses would have to carve out the tablets by himself.

When we are disappointed with God's people, we must avoid the temptation to destroy the sacred with the profane, which is easy to do when bitterness takes root. Consider the pastor who possesses a real promise from God for blessing on his church, only to discard those promises when a divisive remnant of people seeks to divide the congregation.

In the heat of the battle, despair and hopelessness can loosen a heart's grip on the promises of God. We must be very careful, for bitterness can so infect us that His promises grow faint and faith is dimmed. If we allow unbelief to shape our thoughts through complaining, criticism, fault finding, then it will be harder to confidently grasp those promises when God wants to make them real again.

The threshold of self-sacrifice

At his third threshold, Moses plumbs a depth to which few have been. Here, he presents God with a counteroffer: "So Moses went back to the LORD and said, 'Oh, what a great sin these people have committed! They have made themselves gods of gold. But now, please forgive their sin—but if not, then blot me out of the book you have written'" (Exodus 32:31–32).

Moses' offer here is not one of merely identifying with the people. No, he was actually offering himself *as a substitute*. He was willing to make atonement—with himself as sacrificial lamb.

This third threshold points to the Cross itself. Carrying the cross means many things, but there is a sense that God calls us to bear the consequences of others' mistakes. Once Moses recovers from the anger that led him to break the tablets, he announces to the people, "I will go up to the LORD: perhaps I can make atonement for your sin" (Exodus 32:30). What transpires next between Moses and God takes us terrifyingly close to the smoking chasm of self-sacrifice—where love is shaped by humility's demands, where faith is summoned by suffering, where a king becomes a baby and a cross becomes a throne, and where hell is invaded for a heavenly purpose.

Moses offers God an all-or-nothing proposition. Because he knew the consequence of an eternity without God, a debate must have raged within him: *Should I go through with this?* But face-to-face with God again, he cries out, "Please forgive their sin—but if not, then blot me out of the book you have written" (Exodus 32:32). Amazing!

When Moses climbs back up the mountain, he knows full well that God requires a lamb for an atoning sacrifice. Yet he goes empty handed, willing to be the sacrifice for his people, the substitute for their sin and rebellion. One by one, Moses lays down his dreams and God's promises, much as Abraham had done with his son Isaac. All Moses hopes for, all he envisions—he lays it all down.

What does this say to us about bearing the consequences of others' faults, mistakes, and sins? That we need to patiently endure the sins of others, including those sins committed against us. For example, when we allow someone to vent his anger in our direction, while we remain kind and open hearted, we give that person the emotional release he or she may need to find Jesus. In this sense, we become a scapegoat—one on whom blame is laid—and that can set the stage for reconciliation later on.

None of us will be called to exchange our eternal salvation for the sake of another (though the apostle Paul said in Romans 9:3 that he was certainly willing to do so for the sake of the Jews). But the pathway to God's glory leads to this: sacrificing our dreams—and ourselves, if necessary—that others might find freedom. Know this: Moses would not have heard the Lord say, "Lead the people to the place I spoke of" if he hadn't embraced this cross.

And there Moses was. The last time he heard God, He wanted to destroy the people. Then Moses had descended the mount, and judgment had been executed. Three thousand people now lay dead, and the fledgling nation was at a standstill.

It was Moses' willingness to die to his dreams and plead for his people that got them going again.

The threshold of His presence

In Exodus 33:1–3, Moses faces yet a fourth threshold, the presence of God Himself: "Then the LORD said to Moses, 'Leave this place, you and the people you brought up out of Egypt, and go up to the land I promised on oath to Abraham, Isaac, and Jacob, saying, "I will give it to your descendants." I will send an angel before you and drive out [your enemies]. Go up to the land flowing with milk and honey. But I will not go with you, because you are a stiff-necked people and I might destroy you on the way.'"

Moses' journey to the revelation of God's glory brought a more subtle challenge. God promised to protect and bless Moses and the people. He told Moses He would send His angel with them, drive out their enemies, bring them into a land flowing with milk and honey, and grant them prosperity. Any of us would be amazed at such a commitment from God. No doubt Moses breathed a sigh of relief, knowing that God would make good on His promises.

But though God pledged to keep His promise, He denied them His presence. Moses knew that this was not enough, and he told the Lord: "If your Presence does not go with us, do not send us" (Exodus 33:15).

Fulfilled promises without the Father's presence can be devastating. Moses knew that to settle for God's promise without His presence would leave the people detached from the very One who was able to sustain them once they entered the Promised Land. Unless they cultivated an appetite for His presence now, they would have no spiritual stamina to steward the land later. Nothing is so potentially destructive as a land flowing with milk and honey. Only a hunger for His presence can sustain us even when the promises are fulfilled. Likewise, nothing can so ultimately erode our zeal for the Lord like enjoying His blessing apart from a genuine relationship with Him.

Knowing God's blessing without knowing His presence can

retard our spiritual maturity. Blessing alone turns the innocence of childlike dependence into the irresponsible behavior of a spoiled juvenile. Contentment with His blessings without an appetite for His presence can be one of the most dangerous of all deceptions, for we can take His blessing as a sign of approval while ignoring areas where our lives are slowly being polluted.

In many ways we are like my eight-year-old daughter. Words can't describe the exhilaration I feel when this excited little girl in a ponytail—eager to see her daddy—meets me at the airport when I return home after a lengthy trip. It's enough to make a dad feel like a sultan. But sometimes I'm not sure that it's just me she's doing cartwheels over. "Did you bring me a present?" she asked me when I returned recently from a trip. Yes, she was glad to have me home, but she was more interested in what I was going to give her.

Aren't we often like a child waiting to see if her father has brought a present—more interested in what God does for us than in who He is? When the pressure's on, we want solutions more than a sense of His presence. We want *answers from* God, rather than *glimpses of* God.

Moses wisely sought God's presence, but what exactly was he looking for? Didn't he already possess the inner sense of security that God was blessing him? Yes, but the sense that he belonged to God was not enough for him.

Recently, while flying to Detroit, I had a chat with a young college freshman enrolled at University of California-Davis. He was heading home for the holidays, and boy was he looking forward to a huge dose of family! Studying more than two thousand miles away did not jeopardize his *standing* with his family, nor did it undermine the *security* he felt as a son of parents he knew loved him. But knowing that he was their son and relaxing in the security of their love was not enough. He wanted face-to-face time!

And that's what Moses wanted. Yet even here, Moses was not satisfied. For he knew there was something beyond His *promises,* something even beyond His *presence.*

THE PINNACLE OF GLORY

God must have been deeply satisfied with Moses' desire to possess not just the benefits of His promises but also the beauty of His presence. Moved by Moses' response, God says, "I will do the very thing you have asked, because I am pleased with you and I know you by name" (Exodus 33:17).

Surely possessing the presence of the Lord is the height of spiritual intimacy. But having received God's guarantee of the surety of His presence, Moses—in a gush of spontaneous desire—cries out to see God's glory (v. 18). This must have touched something deep in the heart of Father God. Here was a man who was not content with God's promises and not even content with His presence—Moses wanted His glory!

What was Moses asking for? Had he not seen the majesty of God's glory? Had he not witnessed firsthand the deliverance of a people from the mightiest power on earth? Had he not watched in astonishment as the sea parted and the people move forward on dry land? Hadn't he seen Mt. Sinai erupt with the awesome display of God's power? Hadn't he just been in communion with God as he received the law written by His very finger?

What was Moses asking for? I believe he was telling God, "I don't want just Your presence. I want *You!*" More than simply wanting the security of having God close by, Moses wanted to penetrate the depths of God's heart.

When Moses asked to see the Lord's glory, He must have been moved in a way He had never been moved. Here was man who wanted more than the benefit of His promises, more than the security of His presence—he wanted God's heart. It was as if Moses was saying, "God, I want to know what makes You God. I want to know what is in Your heart. Show me what You are really like."

Moses was after more than just a display of supernatural power; he wanted to know what motivated God at the deepest levels of His being. For His part, God must have been pleased, for rare was the opportunity for Him to be so open with a man as He was with Moses that day. So He hid Moses in the crack of a large boulder and covered him with His hand as He revealed His awesome radiance (Exodus 33:21–23). Moses was stunned with wonder. No wonder he came down the mountain the second time with not just the law in his hands, but the shining of God in his face. He had seen the glory of the Lord and found that place of contentment where, in the face of the bitterest circumstance, the deepest heartbreak, or even the most glorious destiny, He is enough.

CHAPTER 15

The unquenchable flame

The greatest revelation in the Scriptures occurs when the saints, upon seeing Jesus, cast down their crowns before His feet—because they realize when they see Him that they didn't earn those crowns at all.

JOHN CASTEEL

The ocean breeze wafting over me as I shuffled through the sand seemed the most delicious I had ever known. Hawaii's tropical heat and the sweet smell of plumeria would have been intoxicating most days, but this day my heart sang for a different reason.

For seven long years, my wife, Nancy, and I had tried to have children. Our journey, like that of thousands of other childless couples, had been a roller-coaster ride. After so many years and so many disappointments, we had all but lost hope. We married young and began trying to conceive within a couple years. When one year turned to two without success, I found myself discouraged but far from hopeless. For I had recently felt strongly that we were going to have a son.

But that son never came. Two years turned to four. We were only in our midtwenties, but a deep sense of despondency began gnawing at us. By that time, though, we were in the hands of one of the best infertility specialists in California, and we were told we would never have kids, that we were in the 2 percent of couples with whom nothing physically wrong could be detected but for whom conception was all but impossible.

Again I went to prayer. Again the Lord impressed on me that we *were* going to have a son. But this time, He added a bit more detail. "You will have a son when you are thirty," I felt the Father say.

That encounter had been four years earlier. Doubt had plagued us more than once.

But this morning, looking out from the Kona Coast on the bluest ocean I had ever seen, a blanket of holy satisfaction enveloped me. Moments earlier we had received the news: Nancy was pregnant. After years of waiting, it was a little hard to absorb. I was going to be a father.

Yet, as wonderful as that was, something far more exhilarating held me in awe. My son would be born when I was thirty— *just as God had said*. As I reflected on our long journey, my deepest joy was not over the coming birth of our child, but over the fellowship with God along the way—the proving of His faithfulness, the listening to His voice.

He had said when I turned thirty I would be a father. And against all odds, His word was coming true. My heavenly Father knew me by name and had promised me something in detail— and my heart was dancing with His on that beach.

What a joy it is to know the Creator of the countless galaxies, the great Sovereign who knows every sparrow and numbers every grain of sand! In a world of billions of people, this God so wants to be known by one man and by one woman that He walks side by side with them through their childless years.

The golden-mouthed, fourth-century preacher John Chrysostom once said, "God's exceeding desire to be loved comes from loving exceedingly." God's passion for his children to know and love Him cannot be contained in all of heaven. Perhaps that is why He created such a large universe. It is His grand illustration of the size of His love. Maybe that's why David exclaimed that His love reaches to the highest heavens (Psalm 36:5). Maybe that is why the Scriptures declare that as far as the east is from the west, so far has He removed our sin (Psalm 103:12). The vastness of the universe is His artwork of affection to us.

Yet many of us are so busy, so distracted, so anxious about so much.

In the second chapter of the Song of Solomon, the bride finds herself quite suddenly alone. She has been so caught up in all that the Bridegroom has been doing that she never notices that He has slipped away. Wine is flowing in abundance, and a menu of delights pirouettes around her. She is at peace…maybe *too* at peace. For in the midst of all the blessing, her Beloved has bid her to come away with Him. But she has "settled." She has decided that she has gone far enough in her spiritual quest. So when the Master's voice whispered to her, she could not hear. His words were drowned out by the very blessings He had lavished on her, but which had imperceptibly arrested her focus. She is now preoccupied. Settled. Sedated.

All at once she calls…but He does not answer.

She tosses and turns on her bed in feverish anxiety. "I must have Him," she cries. Her despondency steels into a holy resolve. She will have Him no matter what the cost, for without Him she has nothing. She rekindles her flame of desire for Him, and when she finds Him, she seizes Him and *will not let Him go!*

That is why He was silent in the first place. It was but His love wooing her to abandon all competing affections.

She had to come to that place. Beyond the succor of human friendship, beyond the elation of her individual destiny, beyond the comfort of the boundaries of peace she had set for herself. She found what the preacher of Ecclesiastes found: All is emptiness. But to her, the realization that all was empty was her first step to real freedom. Once convinced that there was nothing but emptiness apart from her Beloved, she finds her fullness.

So many times it seems that God rekindles the flame of holy desire in the twilight hours of a soul's refining—when the brooding gray of disappointment threatens to engulf us in a permanent night of hopelessness. Yet in these dusks, God shapes destiny by making us desperate for Him. Creating that exquisite ache that prods us to seek Him at all costs. Tenderly unwrapping all the bandages we've layered over our unhealed hearts.

It was again a time in my life when the passion for the Lord burned low. And as I had done so many times before, I cried out to Him in song:

I'd like to stay and just be friends
   Not have to care about a world that sees its end
It seems that I have a one-track mind
   Measuring my time by fruit that is divine
Rekindled flames
   It seems so right to buy and sell
Do all the normal things that gently lead to hell
   The drink that fills I find is still

Doing Father's will with joy and godly zeal
    Rekindled flames
Yet day by day I feel the weight
    Of petty lies that make me stumble in my race
On you I've set my face
    Awake my soul, loose every chain
And let the fire of God rekindle vision's flame
    Sear my thoughts with your sweet cross
Until I'll never be the same
    Rekindled flames[1]

Come, Lord Jesus, in these days of quiet desperation.

These days when we are accosted from

all sides with a cacophony of voices,

each seeking to draw us away from Your face.

Let not my heart become cold because

of neglect of communion with You;

let not my heart remain bruised because I want to nurse my

wounds more than I want to learn of Your love;

let not my heart be divided by desiring anything but Your glory.

The days are evil, but each minute can be

alive with adventure if I'm wholly Yours.

Let the fire of Your love sweep over my soul like a prairie fire!

Rush the walls of my heart!

Break down any resistance to Your will in me.

And as the days become years and I have run my race,

I will comprehend then, in a way that

I cannot fully comprehend now,

that You were and always will be my unquenchable Flame.

NOTES

CHAPTER 1

1. "Oh, I Want to Know You More" words and music by Steve Fry. Copyright © 1983 Birdwing Music/BMG Songs, Inc. (administered by EMI Christian Music Publishing). All rights reserved. Used by permission.

2. Christopher Lasch, *The Culture of Narcissism: American Life in an Age of Diminishing Expectation* (New York: W. W. Norton, 1978).

3. Henri J. M. Nouwen, *The Way of the Heart* (New York: Ballantine Books, 1981), 39.

4. S. D. Gordon, *Quiet Talks on Prayer* (New York: Fleming H. Revell, 1904), 161–2.

CHAPTER 2

1. Traditionally, the incense has been understood allegorically as the prayers of the saints. This is biblically tenable, although if one examines the text in Revelation 8:3–4, there appears to be a differentiation between the incense and the prayers ("The smoke of the incense, *together* with the prayers of the saints…"). Certainly the concept of prayer broadly defined as communion with God can be understood as incense before Him. But for many prayer is seen more as petition than adoration. We need to make this distinction lest prayer be perceived as a resource for our needs rather than the contemplation of His wonder. In Revelation 5:8, in which prayer is typified as incense,

the context makes it clear that the harp and bowl are closely related. The "incense of prayer" is actually an expression of praise.

2. The Hebrew word *shachah* is first used in Genesis 18:2, referring to Abraham bowing before his heavenly guests. But the context does not fully reveal the concept of worship as the Genesis 22 passage does. For those who conclude that Job was the first book written, the word is found in Job 1:20. But like Genesis 22:5, the context is one of extreme pain. After losing his entire estate and all his children, Job falls down and worships!

3. Vivian Hibbert, *Prophetic Worship* (Dallas, Tex.: Cuington Press, 1999), 74.

4. The word is used in Deuteronomy 18:5 and 7 and is meant to convey the worship of Yahweh by calling upon Him.

5. Hibbert, *Prophetic Worship,* 81.

6. Many models are given in Scripture that are designed to aid us in our communion with God. Perhaps the most important model is the Lord's Prayer, or as some more accurately call it, the Believer's Prayer. Beginning with the declaration of our security in God as our Father, this prayer leads us step by step in worship, supplication, confession, and finally praise. Psalm 100 is yet another model—here we are summoned to enter His gates with thanksgiving and enter His courts with praise. The very tabernacle design itself gives us one of the best models to follow in our devotional times with God. The model in Ezekiel 44 is helpful in showing us how to enter into His presence.

7. F. B. Meyer, as heard in a lecture.

CHAPTER 3

1. Gordon Fee, *Paul, the Spirit, and the People of God* (Peabody, Mass.: Hendrickson Publishers, 1996), 15.

2. As quoted in Richard Foster, James Bryan Smith, eds., *Devotional Classics* (San Francisco: HarperCollins, 1993), 173.

3. Jill Haak Adels, *The Wisdom of the Saints—An Anthology* (Oxford: Oxford University Press, 1987), 37.

4. Richard Foster, *Celebration of Discipline* (New York: Harper & Row, 1978), 147.

CHAPTER 4

1. The Song, though it is an erotic love poem, has been seen for centuries as an allegory of the love between God and His people. The poem can be read as a play with three principle characters (the King, the shepherd-bridegroom, and the bride) or simply as the tale of a bride and bridegroom. My interpretation follows the latter.

2. Rabbi Levi Ben Gershom (1288–1344), one of Judaism's most intriguing figures, brings a rich understanding to this text. Levi Ben Gershom, *Commentary on Song of Songs,* trans. by Menachem Kellner (New Haven, Conn.: Yale University Press, 1998), 24.

3. Andrew Murray, *Waiting on God* (Minneapolis, Minn.: Bethany House, 1986), 137.

4. C. S. Lewis, *The Problem of Pain* (New York: Macmillan, 1965), 35.

5. Robert Ellsberg, *All Saints: Daily Reflections on Saints, Prophets, and Witnesses for Our Time* (New York: Crossroad, 1997), 561.

6. Richard Foster, James Bryan Smith, eds., *Devotional Classics* (San Francisco: HarperCollins, 1993), 34–5.

CHAPTER 5

1. Steven Fry, *I Am: The Unveiling of God* (Sisters, Ore.: Multnomah Publishers, 2000), 213–5.

2. For a more in-depth perspective on the relationship between worship and God's presence and rule in our lives see Jack Hayford's *Worship His Majesty* (Ventura, Calif.: Regal Books, 2000), 39–43, 125–7.

3. Steven Fry, *I Am: The Unveiling of God*, 23.

4. A. W. Tozer, *Worship: The Missing Jewel of the Evangelical Church*, as quoted in *Best of A. W. Tozer* (Grand Rapids, Mich.: Baker Book House, 1978), 219.

5. *Day by Day with the Early Church Fathers*, ed. by Christopher D. Hudson, J. Alan Sharrer, Lindsay Vanker (Peabody, Mass.: Hendrickson Publishers, 1999), 48.

CHAPTER 6

1. Dan Sneed, *The Power of a New Identity* (Tonbridge, Kent, UK: Sovereign World, 2000), 67.

2. Dallas Willard, *The Divine Conspiracy*, (San Francisco: Harper San Francisco, 1998), 315.

3. Hannah Whitall Smith, *The Christian's Secret of a Happy Life* (Old Tappan, NJ: Fleming H. Revell, 1970), 32.

4. Richard Foster, *Celebration of Discipline* (New York: Harper & Row, 1978), 22.

5. Ibid., 15.

6. Campbell McAlpine, *Alone with God: A Manual of Biblical Meditation* (Minneapolis, Minn.: Bethany House, 1981), 75.

7. *Spirit Filled Bible*, (Nashville, Tenn.: Thomas Nelson, 1991), 753.

8. Campbell McAlpine, *Alone with God,* 17.

9. Ibid., 68.

10. A. W. Tozer, *The Divine Conquest* (Harrisburg, Penn.: Christian Publications, 1950), 81.

11. McAlpine, *Alone with God,* 78.

12. Thomas Cahill, *How the Irish Saved Civilization* (New York: Doubleday, 1995), 13.

13. Paul Johnson, *The Quest for God* (New York: Harper & Collins, 1996), 202.

CHAPTER 7

1. As quoted by Paul Billheimer in *Destined for the Throne* (Fort Washington, Penn.: Christian Literature Crusade, 1975), 51.

2. As quoted by David Watson in *Called and Committed* (Wheaton, Ill.: Shaw Publishers, 1982), 83.

3. P. T. Forsythe, *Giant Steps*, ed. Warren W. Wiersbe (Grand Rapids, Mich.: Baker Books, 1981), 234.

4. Richard Lovelace, *The Dynamics of Spiritual Life: An Evangelical Theology of Renewal* (Downers Grove, Ill.: IVP, 1980), 159–60.

5. Calvin Miller, *The Table of Inwardness* (Downers Grove, Ill.: InterVarsity Press, 1984), 69.

C H A P T E R   8

1. As quoted by Dallas Willard, *Hearing God* (Downers Grove, Ill.: InterVarsity Press, 1999), 16.

2. As quoted by David Manning White in *The Search for God* (New York: Macmillan, 1983), 178.

3. Willard, *Hearing God,* 22.

4. *Western Asceticism,* ed. Owen Chadwick (Philadelphia: Westminster Press, 1958), 151.

C H A P T E R   9

1. Ken Gire, *Windows of the Soul* (Grand Rapids, Mich.: Zondervan, 1996), 17.

2. Dallas Willard, *Hearing God* (Downers Grove, Ill.: InterVarsity Press, 1984), 57.

3. Oswald Chambers, *My Utmost for His Highest,* (New York: Dodd, Mead, and Co., 1935), 4.

4. Hannah Whitall Smith, *The Christian's Secret of a Happy Life* (Old Tappan, NJ: Revell, 1970), 73.

5. Garth Lean, *On the Tail of a Comet: The Life of Frank Buchman* (Colorado Springs, Colo.: Helmers & Howard, 1988), 74–5.

CHAPTER 10

1. F. Delitzsch, *Commentary on the Old Testament, Vol. 5: Psalms* (Grand Rapids, Mich.: Eerdmans), 97. This Hebrew word for *clap* is often translated "blow," as in the blasting of a trumpet.

2. A different Hebrew word than is used in Psalm 47:1, but the militaristic sense is similar.

3. Richard Foster, *Celebration of Discipline* (New York: Harper & Row, 1978), 147.

CHAPTER 11

1. The Hebrew word for *setting* in 28:13 is translated *tambourine* in Jeremiah 31:4 and Psalm 81:2.

2. Basilea Schlink, *The Unseen World of Angels and Demons* (Basingstoke, UK: Lakeland Press, 1985), 10.

3. Eddie Gibbs, in his book *I Believe in Church Growth,* discusses the way Israel understood her mission. Clearly, she saw herself as being a showcase of a people under Yahweh's rule and enjoying His presence. The rule and presence of Yahweh reached the apex of its national expression under David.

4. John Binns, *Ascetics and Ambassadors of Christ: The Monasteries of Palestine, 314–631* A.D. (Oxford, UK: Clarendon Press, 1994), 239–41.

CHAPTER 12

1. Leonard Sweet, *Post Modern Pilgrims: Post Modern Passion for the 21st Century World* (Nashville, Tenn.: Broadman & Holman, 2000), 56.

CHAPTER 13

1. "Oh, the Glory of His Presence" words and music by Steve Fry. Copyright © 1983 Birdwing Music/BMG Songs, Inc. (administered by EMI Christian Music Publishing). All rights reserved. Used by permission.
2. David McCullough, *The Trivialization of God: The Dangerous Illusion of a Manageable Deity* (Colorado Springs, Colo.: Navpress, 1995), 81.
3. As quoted by David Watson, *Called and Committed* (Wheaton, Ill.: Harold Shaw Publishers, 1982), 10.
4. *Creation in Christ,* ed. Rolland Hein (Wheaton, Ill.: Harold Shaw Publishers, 1976), 159.

CHAPTER 14

1. Gerald Fry, *In Pursuit of His Glory: A Quest to Know the Power and Presence of God* (Tacoma, Wash.: Mt. Hermon Ministries, 1999), 7–9. Copies of this book may be obtained by calling 253-460-1162, faxing 253-460-1182, or e-mailing G.L.Fry@juno.com.

CHAPTER 15

1. "Rekindled Flame" words and music by Steve Fry. Copyright © 1985 Deep Fryed Music. All rights reserved.

Multnomah Publishers

The publisher and author would love to hear your
comments about this book. *Please contact us at:*
www.multnomah.net/rekindledflame

OUR WORSHIP OF GOD IS ONLY AS DEEP AS OUR KNOWLEDGE OF HIM...

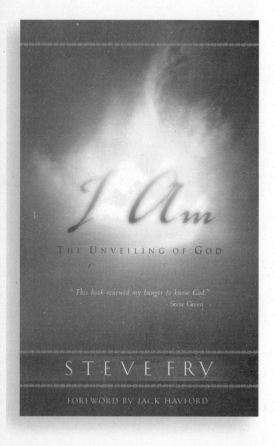

Discover the many facets of God in this unique, affordable collection of forty faith-building essays and stories. An honest, candid prayer is included at the end of each chapter—as well as questions for further meditation.

ISBN 1-57673-690-3

"If you know Steve Fry mainly for his acclaimed musicals *We Are Called* and *Thy Kingdom Come*, you will be completely taken aback by the fresh and totally contemporary sounds of this worship collection…. Spiritually, the quality of lyrics impresses me just as much as the actual music that carries the lyrics. Powerful but simple truths simply jump out of every song."

—TOM LENNIE OF GOLD USA

"Steven is one of those writer/artists whose passionate pursuit of the Savior never ceases to leave me desiring to know God's heart more fully and experience His grace more deeply. Once again Steven has crafted a wonderful musical and lyrical invitation to draw near to the throne of the Living God."

—STEVEN CURTIS CHAPMAN

The CD *Rekindled Flame* is the companion
to Steve Fry's book *Rekindled Flame*.

To order your copy of the CD *Rekindled Flame*,
call **Steven Fry Ministries: (615) 370-1322** or
visit his **Web site: www.stevenfryministries.com.**